SWITCHING ON *the* HEAVENS

Harnessing the Power of Prayer for Victorious Living

SWITCHING ON *the* HEAVENS

Harnessing the Power of Prayer for Victorious Living

Victor M. Sulaiman

WORD2PRINT

A Division of One-Touch UK

SWITCHING ON THE HEAVENS

First published in the United Kingdom in 2014 by Word2Print for Church Reformation Movement (CRM) Publishing House
ISBN 978-1-908588-09-8

Produced for CRM Books by Word2Print

www.word2print.com

A CIP catalogue record for this title is available from the British Library

Printed by CPI Group (UK), Croydon CR0 4YY

Table of Contents

Dedication

I would like to dedicate this book to my Lord and Saviour Jesus Christ, my lovely wife and children for their love, support and dedication for the work of the ministry.

Introduction

PRAYER IS A common spiritual exercise but a delicate and complex spiritual task. Nearly every human prays in one way or the other, in different forms, at different places, and at different times. I have even heard the so-called atheists say 'God help me'. If the estimated 2.2 billion Christians around the world pray once per day, God would have 2.2 billion prayer requests to deal with each day and that would be too small for Him to answer. What an amazing God we serve! What a great impact the Church around the world will make if all believers find time to pray each day for the salvation and healing of the world. But this is not the case.

Majority of Christians find it difficult to pray. Some believe that their pastor will pray for them or that the 'big men of God' must pray for them. Prayer should be a 'do-it-yourself' exercise. If all Christians pray rightly, it will change the world for the better. The most common prayer you will hear most of the time is 'God bless you', 'O God, have mercy', 'O God, help me', or the traditional grace said after every Church service. These type of prayers become.s a form of habit; mere expressions of the lips, when people are in serious danger or a threatening situation. Prayer however is deeper, powerful and more effective than you might think. It is one of the most powerful legacies that Jesus gave to His Church before He left the world.

Switching on the Heavens has been written out of the passion to inform Christians about the need to adopt a prayerful lifestyle that will change individual lives, families, communities and the world for good. Christians must begin to see prayer as a means of communion, communication, clarification, cancellation, confirmation, care and conclusion of matters with God. It is time you begin to see prayer as a means of actualising God's plans and purposes. Prayer is not just presenting request lists to God, but a medium of receiving revelations about your needs and what God's plans for your future are. This book will help you to see prayer as not just asking something from God but giving one's whole life to God; not just praying to God but praying with God who dwells in your heart by His Spirit. Prayer is not just an abstract spiritual exercise as some people think; it is a Father-son relationship; a conversation between two real people.

You will read in this book about the types of communication when praying. Most of the time, your prayers may involve a one-way communication, where you express your needs, believing God for answers but not giving God time to communicate with you. You will learn how God uses verbal, written and sign communication to express His will to you in prayer. Many visions and dreams may have come to you in the past but you never took them seriously, tried to understand what you saw or heard, or acted on them for effective results. You will come to realise that you can receive this communication through the Word of God, dreams or visions.

This book reveals to you that prayer is not only engaging with the devil in a spiritual fight but engaging God and His Word and tactics to defeat the devil. There is no real deliverance or spiritual warfare without the right spiritual weapons. Apostle Paul advises us to put on the whole armour of God (Ephesians 6:10-11). Prayer is not a militant or emotional exercise. It is a spiritual meditation with the aim of getting into the heart of God through His Word and Spirit. Prayer enables you to know God's will for your life and situation. In this book, you will get to know how the prayer giants of the Bible - Moses, Joshua, Hannah, Elijah, Daniel, Jesus and the early Church believers used the power of prayer to switch on the heavens and change their world. You too can bring uncommon change to your world today through the power of prayer.

Victor Sulaiman
London, June 2014

Acknowledgements

FIRST I LIKE to thank God Almighty who answers all prayers, who saved my soul, who has given me wisdom, knowledge, understanding, the revelation of His word and endowed me with His grace to pray and preach His Word. I thank Him for seeing me through various challenges of life and teaching me to experience His divine presence and love all the time.

I will forever be indebted to men and women of God who have assisted in reading the drafts of this book at every stage. I wish to acknowledge the support I received from Dr Muyiwa Olumoroti, Motunrayo Ade-Famoti, Gbenga Olorunleye, Daniel Lanre and Emily Sulaiman. You have contributed immensely to the preparation of this book. You are all to me 'up lifter of holy hand and voice' in the wilderness.

I also wish to acknowledge the skillful assistance that I received from the staff of Word2Print Publishing in the final production of this book. Thank you all for your encouragement and support all the way. May the Lord bless you and answer your prayers in an awesome way.

Chapter 1

The Meaning of Prayer

THEWORD 'PRAYER' is common to people but its real meaning is not. The word 'prayer' in Hebrew, (Tepilla) means intercession, supplication, or a hymn. The word 'prayer' in Greek, (Proseuche) means prayer, worship, or earnest prayer. This word occurs 85 times in the Old Testament and about 53 times in the New Testament of the Bible. Prayer is a deeper relationship with God - a communication, a dialogue, an expression, and a conversation between humanity and his or her Maker. It is a link between the creation and the creator of the universe. It is a spiritual affair, a spiritual warfare, a spiritual communion, and a spiritual exchange of views between man and God.

"The greatest lack today is not people, funds, philosophy, theology, pastors or churches. The greatest lack today is prayer. The task of prayer needs to be multiplied in order to meet the spiritual needs of today's world."

According to Billy Graham the great man of God, 'prayer is spiritual communication between man and God, a two way communication and relationship in which man should not only talk to God but also listen to Him. Prayer to God is like a child's communication with his father. It is natural for a child to ask his father for the things he needs'. Prayer is a spiritual affair and not a natural affair as God has no natural form. Jesus declared that God is a Spirit, and His worshippers must worship Him in spirit and in truth (John 4:24). To engage God in prayer, you need to graduate from the natural to spiritual. What is born of the flesh is flesh and what is born of the Spirit is spirit. Prayer therefore is a spiritual exercise to bring into the realm of the physical what is ordained in the spirit. The task of prayer is that of God's Spirit.

You can't pray effectively without God's Spirit in you. You need God's Spirit to hear God speaking to you in prayer.

Dr Myles Munroe once defined prayer as 'man giving God the legal right and permission to interfere in earth affairs. Prayer is the heavenly licence to influence the earth; a terrestrial licence for celestial interference. Prayer is man exercising his legal authority on earth to invoke heaven's influence on the planet.' (Myles Munro, Understanding Prayer, page 14).' Prayer is an open door between you and God, a connection between the Creator and the creation, where views, plans and purposes are exchanged. Prayer is your spiritual right to enter into the realm of God; your spiritual right to declare what has been written in heaven on earth, and your spiritual authority to cancel whatever works against God's ordained purposes. Like Prophet Elijah, you have a legal right through God's Spirit to switch on or switch off the heavens.

David Yonggi Cho, the pastor of the largest Church in South Korea, believes that 'prayer is tapping the heavenly power to revive and restore the world back to God's will and purpose.' Nothing happens in the Church without prayer. Anything supernatural can happen in the Church through constant prayer, and prayer is a strong weapon that overturns the enemies' plan and enthrones God's will for His glory.'

Charles Spurgeon defined prayer 'as a covering, a house without prayer is a house without a roof. A house without a roof is an incomplete house and is liable to danger, destruction and disaster. Prayer is a connection to the greater power available to us in God's Kingdom. It is the best means of handling the most distressing and depressing situation of human life' (Spurgeon: Spiritual Warfare page 114, 336).

Prayer is not just lip communication; it is a rendering of the heart. It is not lip connection; it is heart connection (Matthew 15:8-9). The main subject in prayer is you and your Creator. Those who seek God in prayer need to examine their hearts whether it is right with God or not. You must connect with God through your heart before you connect Him with your lips. Too many words from an impure heart are a mere noise to God. Therefore, prayer is both heart and lip communication and communion with God.

King David realised that God's requirement in prayer is not a broken head but a broken heart. How you appear outwardly does not guarantee your relationship and answers to prayer. All God needs is the right heart that is humble and one that obey God's instructions. King David in Psalm 100 called attention to the reality of the existence of God that is knowable, reachable and touchable; a God who revealed Himself in creation and in His only begotten Son Jesus Christ and in His care for humanity.

Knowing God is an essential ingredient of faith and prayer; the Psalmist calls for the knowledge of God's person, His creation and His providence. Creation is not the product of nature itself as scientists and evolutionists would like to suggest. The creation flows from the Creator and this came into being by His active and powerful Word (Gen.1:1-26; John 1:1-3).

The goodness and love of God is evidenced in His general and specific revelations. He cares for our physical needs through nature, and our spiritual needs through His Son Jesus Christ. Knowing God better requires revelation through His Word. The only book that gives you the true spiritual nature of God is the Bible. The knowing ability displayed in science, philosophy and all forms of education are the extension of the highest knowledge. Human knowledge can never and will never extend from a lower animal. The message that flows through your mind each second has an origin in God.

Prayer is engaging God in a round table conversation on particular pressing issues, events, plans, visions, problems or purposes. James the Apostle tells us, *"Elijah was a man just like us. He prayed earnestly that it would not rain, and it did not rain on the land for three and a half years. Again he prayed, and the heavens gave rain, and the earth produced its crops"*(James 5:17).A woman once gave her testimony about how she engaged God in prayer over a pressing issue in her life. She said she sat on a chair in her living room at midnight, and gave God another chair, and invited God to come and sit down and listen to her conversation. I asked this woman if she saw God sitting in front of her during her prayer time. She said 'no' but that she saw God by faith and believed that God listens and responds to the prayers of the righteous. This woman saw through the eyes of the spirit that God is always involved in a genuine and sincere prayer.

During the days of Elijah, there was apostasy, idolatry and backsliding. King Ahab took the entire Israel nation into the worship of Baal. Elijah the Prophet engaged God in prayer about what to do to restore Israel back into the worship of the Living God. The Lord told Prophet Elijah what to do to convince Israel that Baal was not the real God. God told Elijah, "You know what? You will have to engage Ahab, the 850 prophets of Baal and the entire Israel in an evening sacrifice on Mount Carmel. Let the prophets of Baal offer their sacrifice first and call on their gods to set their sacrifice on fire. And you will do likewise and call on me and I will answer you by fire. The God that answered by fire is God."

Elijah did as God instructed, and God proved Himself as the only true God. At the time of the sacrifice, Elijah came forward and reminded God of their agreement in prayer: *'O Lord, God of Abraham, Isaac and Israel, let it be known today that you are God in Israel and that I am your servant and have done all these things at your command. Answer me, O Lord, answer me, so these people will know that you, O Lord, are God and that you are turning their hearts back again' (1King 18:36-37).* God responded to Elijah's prayer by fire to confirm His Word and promise to him. Prophet Elijah switched off the power of Baal and his prophets and switched on the heaven of the God of Israel.

Prayer is not just an expression of your opinion about issues, problems, and difficulties with God. It is sharing views of His promises, written and revealed through His Son Jesus Christ. Prayer is declaring the authority of God's Word and His revelation on any situation mitigating against God's purposes.

Just as children grow through relationship with their parents, prayer is a relationship that sparks spiritual growth that helps you to hear God speaking His will into your heart. It is a relationship that grows you into a person in whom the Spirit of God takes charge of your prayer life. This book is to inspire all believers into this type of relationship. When you stop praying, the Spirit of God stops speaking to you until you re-open your conversation with Him again. This is why Paul the Apostle advises us that we should pray always (1 Thessalonians 5:17).

POINTS ON PRAYER

- Prayer is a spiritual exercise to bring into the realm of the physical what is ordained in the spirit.
- Prayer is man giving God the legal right and permission to interfere in earth affairs.
- Prayer is a relationship that sparks spiritual growth that helps you to hear God speaking His will into your heart.

Chapter 2

Why You Need to Pray

SOMEPEOPLEBELIEVE that they don't need to pray because God is their Father, the Creator of Heaven and Earth, the giver of life and everything in this world. Prayer to some people, (often rich, happy and wealthy people) is like a waste of time. Some even ask: "Why should I waste my time in prayer if I can get what I need?" One of the challenges facing the Church today is that many people don't see the necessity of praying anymore as almost everything is becoming within reach or free (housing, transport, welfare, medical services, education). I thought the same way as a young believer but let us look at prayer and get an insight from the Bible.

Naturally, conversation and communication is part of the creative arrangement of the Almighty God. Humans express their will, desire, and ideas through various communication processes. The sharing of information, knowledge or ideas would not have been possible if there were no mechanisms to communicate. Children enjoy parent's provision and love through communication. Meaningful relationship will not be possible if there were no conversation. Nature depends and benefits from the constant flow of conversation. Continents are linked together now with 24 hours news network. The world is being transformed through conversation and communication. Knowledge is being passed from one generation to the other to improve standards of living through meaningful communication of useful ideas. The will of humanity is expressed in the form of conversation and communication.

Communication is not limited to nature alone; communication is also going on constantly in the spirit realm. King David declared that

"The heavens declare the glory of God; the skies proclaim the work of his hands. Day after day they pour forth speech; night after night they display knowledge"

-Psalm 19:1-2

If heavens declare the glory of God each day, it implies that what each day brings to humanity (life, growth, death, sunshine, rain, snow, heat, wind, storm, stars, cloud, day, night) speak for God.

Jesus declared that 'God is Spirit, and his worshippers must worship Him in Spirit and in truth (John 4:24). God is a Spirit being who speaks His eternal intention into all His creation including humans. The world of the Spirit is vital to human existence and fulfilment. There are two domains in life: the spiritual and the physical domain. The latter flows from the former. Both domains are dependent on each other and exist together. The giver of the physical domain gives humans the authority to reign over the physical realm. We are created to exercise dominion over all the works of God. We are to rule, govern, and become head of it all (Psalm 8:1-6; Hebrew 2:6-8; 5:7-8).

The authority to rule and reign over the physical domain was lost to Satan through sin (Genesis 3:1ff). Since then, Satan has taken charge of the physical domain and put humanity under his control. The communication line between the spiritual and the physical domain was cut off when man fell in the Garden of Eden. This is why Jesus told His disciples: *"This is why I speak to them in parables. You will be ever hearing but never understanding, you will be ever seeing but never perceiving, for this people's heart has become calloused; they hardly hear with their ears and they have closed their eyes. Otherwise they might see with their eyes, hear with their ears, understand with their hearts and turn, and I will heal them" (Matthew 13: 14-15).* Since then, there is spiritual conflict between these domains (Ephesians 6:12-18; 2 Corinthians 10:3-6; Luke 4:1-13). Jesus has come therefore to redeem, restore and link these domains back to man.

Like Adam and Eve in the Garden of Eden before the fall, you have the capacity to hear God's voice speaking His eternal mind to you. Communication continues in the spirit realm but the revelation ability given to you was lost through disobedience to God and His Word. You are reconnected to this spiritual realm in conversion, when you repent and change your heart and believe that God exists and He is knowable.

Praying to God all the time invites God into your physical domain. Prayer is asking Him to take charge of certain areas of your life that have been tampered with by satanic influences (Hebrew 2:14). Jesus had to come in human form and die so He could destroy the power of sin and restore us into our original state of authority - to rule and have dominion over the physical realm. When you pray, you are inviting His perfect will, plan and purpose. That invitation is necessary because God will not operate against your will.

What do you think would become of a world where communication and conversation is withdrawn completely? There will be total confusion and chaos. A prayerless life is therefore subjected to crises and commotion at all times. Since God has the best plan for you and will not enforce His plan upon you without asking Him, you are obliged to seek Him in prayer, inviting Him to take control of your physical domain.

In prayer you get to know God's will for your life now and the future. You feel His presence now and every time. You discern His plan now and in the future. You also enthrone His dominion in your life now and in the future (John 15:7; 1 John 5:14). Asking what you need and asking according to His will is crucial in your life and the life of the Church today. How do you discern what you want or need in the light of God's will? Accessing and aligning your needs is therefore vital to a prevailing prayer life.

God's will was a reference point for Jesus' life, ministry and miracles on earth (John 5:27-30). God depended on Jesus for His will to be fulfilled. This implies that God and Jesus depended on each other for the fulfilment of the divine agenda. Likewise, God depends on you and the Church for the fulfilment of His divine plan on the earth. God depends on those who work within the boundary of His will to fulfil His divine plan. Every believer is therefore sent with a specific duty to perform in both the physical and the spiritual realm. Prayer is therefore inviting God to carry out His will through us on planet earth.

Through prayer, you uncover the knowledge of God and His will for your life, your family, your community, and your nation. Prayer exposes the destructive plan of Satan and gives insight to overturn it with divine pronouncement. God is waiting for your prayers before acting on your behalf in earthly affairs. Prayer invites God into the scene of your life and affairs to display His plan, purpose and power. Prayer is bringing God into the big picture of your life situation. Without divine invitation, there is no divine visitation. God is waiting for your invitation today. When you stop praying you suspend His invitation into your situation. He will not act until you ask (Matthew 7:7-8). Prayer is therefore necessary as the breath of your life!

POINTS ON PRAYER

1. Meaningful relationship will not be possible if there were no conversation.
2. A prayerless life is subjected to crises and commotion at all times.
3. In prayer you get to know God's will for your life now and the future.

Chapter 3

Obstacles to Prayers

THE HINDRANCE TO prayer is generally perceived as sin by many people. Sinners don't pray because they don't have the Spirit of God in them. The task of prayer is spiritual and there is no real prayer without the presence of God's Spirit in your life. Sinners learn to pray for mercy, forgiveness and help when they are convicted of their sins and are willing to repent. However, the first thing that hinders prayer is not praying itself. The intensity of individual prayer determines the intensity of the corporate prayer of a family or the Church. Prayer is the licence and the authority that believers have to interfere with the supernatural. Neglecting prayer therefore disconnects the creation from the Creator. It distance believers from the throne of grace, and severs communication between the Lord and the Church. Eventually this will lead to the advancement of the kingdom of darkness.

Jesus' disciples slept at a time of prayer, not because they were sinners, but because they had not received the Spirit that prays (Matthew 26:40). Apostle Paul advises you to pray continually and to give thanks in all circumstances, which is God's will for you in Christ Jesus. Do not put out the Spirit's fire; do not treat prophecies with contempt, and test everything that is godly and ungodly to hold unto what is true, right and acceptable (1 Thessalonians. 5:17-22). According to Apostle Paul, continuous prayer helps you to form the habit of thanksgiving, increases the Spirit's fire in you, and helps you tap into God's mysteries through revelations. Prayer provides strength in overcoming evil each day. Whenever there is disconnection between God and you, the Spirit is silenced, depression and anxiety take the place of thanksgiving, you become indifferent to prophetic declarations and word of knowledge and the devil inflicts your heart with evil, doubt and deceit.

I must submit that the willingness to pray continually is fast disappearing in the lives of Christians. The experience of Jesus and His disciples at a crucial time of spiritual need supports this view. Jesus asked His disciples to keep watch with Him in prayer for one hour in order to confirm His Father's will at Gethsemane. He came back to find His disciples sleeping. Jesus' disciples' laziness and spiritual dullness are dangerous to the challenges and task ahead of them. Jesus therefore encouraged them to watch and pray so that they would not fall into temptation. When you are tempted to stop praying, you open the back door of temptations into your life. To stop praying therefore is more disastrous than stopping to eat and drink.

I will now consider the other factors that hinder prayer:

1. Knowledge without the practice

Knowing and teaching about prayer is not the same thing as putting prayer into practice. Theological knowledge of prayer or attending school of prayer does not guarantee the ability to pray. Theological divergences on prayer do not inspire theology students to pray or empower them to utilize the power of prayer. Jesus' disciples were in the best 'theological school' of all time, yet they were sleeping when they should be praying. The best school of prayer is the school of the Holy Spirit. One day Jesus' disciples observed that Jesus' prayer life was different from the one they inherited from Jewish religious tradition. So they asked Jesus: *"Teach us how to pray"*(Luke 11:1).

After the disciples received the authoritative lecture from their Master, they forgot to put into practice what they had received when challenges arose at Gethsemane. The knowledge was there, but the will power to put the knowledge into action wasn't. Praying is not the product of head knowledge; it is the force of God's Spirit in you that inspires you to pray. Apostle Paul says: "*We do not know what we ought to pray for, but the Spirit himself intercedes for us with groans that words cannot express"*(Romans 8:26).

Many believers read about men and women of prayer in the Bible but they fail to practise the prayer life these people lived that made them to experience supernatural results. James the Apostle emphasized the importance of a dynamic prayer life with reference to Elijah. He said, "*Elijah was a man just like us. He prayed earnestly that it would not rain, and it did not rain on the land for three and a half years. Again he prayed, and the heavens gave rain, and the earth produced its*crops" (James 5:17-18).

Prayer is therefore a powerful weapon for tapping into God's supernatural resources. Gathering information about available resources is not the same with tapping into the actual resources. Many Christians and pastors who quote this passage to emphasize the importance of prayer in preaching and teaching have not really tapped the resources of prayer like Elijah. Communicating prayer is different from commitment to prayer; and as Myles Munroe says "A major cause of unanswered prayer is our becoming experts in the knowledge of prayer but not masters in the practice of praying" (*Understanding the Purpose and Power of Prayer; page 152).* Elijah was able to overthrow King Ahab on his knees; not with the host of Israel Army or through political violence or anarchy. The Scriptures in your head without the Scriptures in your heart and lifestyle are dangerous to your spiritual and prayer life. It is like knowing traffic signs without using them when you drive. The knowledge of prayer must be applied through constant practice of prayer.

2. Spiritual laziness

Laziness is lack of willingness and zeal to pray. It is neglecting the duty of daily prayer. This lack of zeal for prayer could be caused by busyness, distractions, insecurity, contentment or pleasure. Have you been in a prayer meeting where some people doze off after few minutes? Some Christians even believe that they need to be prayed for by a 'mighty man of God' as if the man of God has the power to answer prayers. Laziness is neglecting the duty of prayer and lack of commitment to a sincere prayer lifestyle. It is living a normal life without frequent fellowship with God. It is like an orphan living within reach of our heavenly Father.

King David had to overcome laziness before he triumphed over life challenges. He said*"Have mercies over me O Lord for I call all day long"* (Psalm 86:3). David never gave up to laziness in his prayer life. The disciples were so lazy and weak that they could not pray with Jesus for just one hour (Matthew 26:40). King David's prayer life of praise, petition, supplication and intercession is recorded in the book of Psalm (1-42). Those who live a prevailing prayer life don't toy with prayer; they take prayer seriously each day. This is why Jesus encourages you to watch and prays so as not to fall into temptation (Matthew 26:41). Apostle Paul admonishes you to pray continually because this is the will of God (1 Thessalonians 5:17).

Laziness is a spiritual disease that needs supernatural cure in the 21st Century Church. During services, there is enough time for praise and worship, time to preach the Word of God, time for team meetings and time to do other social activities but less time for prayer. Some Christians don't know what to pray for when they gather for worship. They are like a patient who stands before the doctor and doesn't know how to express his/her ailment or pain. There is no way the doctor can recommend the correct medication for healing without knowing what the ailment is.

Many Christians, pastors, church workers and leaders are in this awful situation just like Jesus' disciples in Luke 11:1. They are really sick of spending time in prayer unlike Jesus. The disciples came to Jesus and said, "Teacher, we want to pray like you. We have tried it a few times but after few minutes we don't know what to say. How do you do it? What do you say in your prayer time for so long?" The reason why some are so lazy to pray is because they are short of prayer points; they crown their lazy habit by saying God knows what they need or that there is no point in wasting their time in long prayers. But look to what the Scripture says:

"During the days of Jesus' life, He offered prayers and petitions with loud cries and tears to the one who could save him from death, and he was heard because of his reverent submission. Although He was a son, He learned obedience from what He suffered and once made perfect, He became the source of eternal salvation for all who obey Him and was designated by God to be high priest in the order of Melchizedek."

-Hebrew 5:7-8

Many Christians today are defeated because the will power to pay the price of prayer is not part of their normal Christian life. They are vulnerable to tiredness, frustration and hopelessness when they encounter little problems. Jesus did not turn His back on His Father's will. He paid the sacrifice for sin and redemption of the world on the Cross. He sought his Father's confirmation and validation for His suffering and thus saved the world. The threat of the Cross was enough to paralyse the spirit and zeal for praying in Jesus. If Jesus was lazy when He faced death on the Cross, He would have missed the prize. He won the final battle on the Cross through prayer and reverent submission. Jesus endured and could pray for those who nailed Him on the Cross because He saw what they did not see and knew what they did not know.

3. Disobeying God's Word

"But they were disobedient and rebelled against you; they put your law behind their backs. They killed the Prophets, who admonished them in order to turn them back to you; they committed awful blasphemies. So you handed them over to their enemies, who oppressed them."

-Nehemiah 9:26-27

Disobedience has to do with how you live your life in line with the Word of God. You are in a world where everything seems right to individuals, and where wrong moral principles are considered right to some extent. Apostle Paul said that disobedience is the kind of spirit that dwells in the mind; it takes people's mind away from God's Word (Ephesians 2:2). Disobedience is also adapting the Word of God to suit your personal pleasure (Romans 5:19) and reducing moral biblical principles to post-modern moral guides born out human philosophy. Believing the Word of God is not the same as behaving the Word of God. The rate of disobedience is higher now due to the application of post-modern mind in interpreting God's Word. How you live your life has no bearing to your faith nowadays.

If prayer is communication and dialogue with God, you disagree with Him when you disagree with His Word; you cannot have a good and positive relationship with Him when you commune in prayer. Disobedience is also defying, rejecting or rebelling against the Word of God (Nehemiah 9:26) and disobedience is saying "No" to God's instructions. But when you pray, you want God to say "Yes" to your requests. Disobedience takes prayer out of biblical context, and reduces God's will, way and life to your own. This is why most of prayers remain unanswered.

The second key factor stated by Jesus in His prayer curriculum to His disciples is *"Your will be done on Earth as it is in Heaven"* (Matthew 6:10). Jesus informed His disciples that God's will is essential in their prayer life. Disobedience is telling God what to do even when it is contrary to His will and Word. This is why James the Apostle declared " *When you ask, you do not receive, because you ask with wrong motives, that you may spend what you get on your pleasures*" (James 4:3).

4. Sinful Lifestyle

Sin is doing what is physically, socially, morally, and spiritually wrong. There are some things people do that are considered morally wrong such as killing, rape, stealing, lying, deception, dishonesty, abuse, sexual lusts and perversion, and divorce which are considered legal. The wrongs that are legally declared right have taken the Church to the realm of spiritual pollution. Today, what is declared wrong by God in His Word has been declared right in our thinking, in the Church and in society. It is a deception of this generation for us to practise wrong doing and claim that we are children of God, pray to God with sinful lifestyles and expect Him to answer.

God hates sin but not sinners. The Word of God, the Spirit of God and sin do not co-exist. God cannot relate with sin and He cannot accept a sinful lifestyle. John the Apostle declared *"He who does what is sinful is of the devil, because the devil has been sinning from the beginning. No one who is born of God will continue to sin, because God's seed remains in him; he cannot go on sinning, because he has been born of God. This is how we know who the children of God are and who the children of the devil are: anyone who does not do what is right is not a child of God"*(1 John 3:8-10).

John's argument is that true children of God do not live a sinful lifestyle. They have the ability to do what is right with God and neighbours. If a child of God co - habits with sin, he or she can claim to be a child of God but truly belongs to the devil - the father of sin. Any believer can belong to any Church, hold any position, or have any title; if the person practices sin, he or she does not belong to God. The Church of God is not meant for dogs, pigs, snakes or wolves but the sheep. Sin of disobedience is rebellion against the Word of God and it breaks your relationship with Him.

God did not tell you in His Word that you can live as you like when you are saved from your past sin. Some of the social lifestyles of this generation disagree with how the Bible defines you should live your life. However the way you live and what you say in prayer matters to God. The Psalmist declared *'If I had cherished sin in my heart, the Lord would not have listened; but God has surely listened and heard my voice in prayer* (Psalm 66:18-19). Sin separates you from God because He is holy and has no relationship with an unholy lifestyle. Sin erects barrier between you and God.

What of national sin or wrong doing? Aaron led the Israel nation to worship the golden calf when Moses went up to the mountain to meet God (Exodus 32). King Ahab led the children of Israel away from God into idol worshipping (1King 18). King Solomon affirms that righteousness exalts a nation, but sin is a disgrace to any people (Proverb 14:34). One of the tricks of Satan today is to make Christians take the grace of God as a licence for living a sinful life. Some Christian authors even claim that we are saints that can commit sin. Some claim that God's unconditional love covers up for sinful lifestyle. From my biblical understanding, God's love is a universal love but God hates sin and sinful living. He does not accept everything that you do.

If parents cannot condone unruly behaviour from their children, God will not accept any of your wrongdoings. His holy and perfect nature cannot co-exist with ungodliness and wickedness. One of the problems that weakens the prayer life of believers today is that the Church is trying to socialise with the world, blending its lifestyle with the one invented by the 21st Century secular culture. Secular and spiritual Christians differ in the kind of lifestyle they live. If the Church wants to ignite the fire of revival, the starting point is to say 'no' to all forms of ungodliness and worldly passions. The Church needs to live a self-controlled, upright and godly lives in this present age while we await the blessed and glorious appearing of our great God and Saviour, Jesus Christ (Titus 2:11-13).

5. Unforgiving Spirit

One of the easiest sins that you can commit is unforgiveness. It is refusing to forgive someone who does you wrong and nursing hatred and bitterness against people that hurt you. Jesus declared: *"For if you forgive other people when they sin against you, your heavenly Father will also forgive you. But if you do not forgive others their sins, your Father will not forgive your sins"*(Matthew 6:14-15).

Unforgiving spirit hinders your prayers, switch off your heavens and paralyses your prayer life. It is a spirit that Satan is using to separate friends, families, colleagues, churches, communities and nations today. I remember an incident when I disagreed with a friend over certain church matters. I had a dream revelation that this person was cursing me using Psalm 109. When I woke up and meditated on this dream, the Spirit of God said 'Let them curse, I will bless.' Forgive and forget what the person has done to you and pray for him. I continued praying for the person. It is ridiculous to use the Word of God as a destructive weapon against people. You are saved to use the Word of God to save and not to destroy life.

Churches and families are collapsing because believers could not forgive each other over trivial matters. What people do to you is not worse than what Jesus experienced on the Cross. Yet He endured such suffering to wipe out your sin by His precious blood. You must forgive others their sin for Christ sake and for the sake of your prayers. Jesus linked prayer to forgiveness because if you did not forgive people and you are praying to God, you are a sinner who has not repented from your sin. Your prayer cannot be answered because God honours prayers from a pure heart.

King David declared:

"Who may ascend the hill of the Lord? Who may stand in His holy place? The one who has clean hands and a pure heart, who doesn't lift up his soul to an idol or swear by what is false. He will receive blessing from the Lord and vindication from God his saviour. Such is the generation of those who seek Him, who seek your face, O God of Jacob."

-Psalm 24:3-6

Forgiving others helps you to appreciate and value God's forgiveness. It gives you the right frame of mind to relate with God and others, and peace of mind. Forgiveness also heals you from bitterness and hatred. It helps you understand the eternal love of God for you and develop in you the spirit of kindness, compassion and love towards others. Forgiving others helps you to earn God's forgiveness and to enjoy the blessing of forgiveness. Jesus teaches that believers who refuse to forgive people their sins and settle matters among themselves are pagans (Matthew 18:15-17). God will never have relationship with pagans unless they repent.

Sometimes ago, I was told that some boys destroyed our church banner. I reported the incident to the caretaker of the place we use for worship and asked him if he could help me to download the close circuit television tapes to trace the boys. I was planning to report the incident to the police for follow up. The following Sunday, I knelt down in the church to pray. As I was praying, the Spirit of God asked me this question. "If Jesus Christ found these boys, what do you think He would do to them? I didn't get the answer immediately. I kept on praying. Later I heard the voice of the Holy Spirit within me saying 'He would invite them for cups of tea and preach the gospel to them. This revelation changed my plan, and I prayed for the boys and I forgot about the incident. You must learn to forgive others no matter what they have done to you so that nothing hinders your prayers.

6. Lack of Faith

Lack of faith simply means lack of belief or doubt. It means not believing in yourself, not believing in your prayer or not believing in God that you are praying to. The Scripture says:

> ***"And without faith it is impossible to please God, because anyone who comes to Him must believe that He exists and that He rewards those who earnestly seek him" (Hebrew 11:6). Jesus said: "Have faith in God. I tell you the truth, if anyone says to this mountain, go, throw yourself into the sea, and do not doubt in his heart but believe that what he says will happen, it will be done for him. Therefore I tell you, whatever you ask for in prayer, believe that you received it, and it will be yours."***
>
> ***-Mark 11:22-24***

There are three voices that speak to you in prayer - the voice of the problems you are praying about (which Jesus likened to a mountain), the voice of your mind (which is what you think or feel about your problems), and the voice of God through His Word or His Spirit. Lack of faith causes your mind to magnify your problems and makes you think that the problems cannot be solved. When you pray and believe in what your problems tell you than what the Word of God says or what God tells you about the problems, you have no faith in God, and your prayer will never be answered. When you pray and you believe in the Word of God or what God says about your problems rather than what your problems are saying, you will receive answers to your prayer. Belief in the existence of God and faith that He can do all things is the power of your prayer life.

Some years ago, we were in a prayer fellowship and a lady came to the church with crutches, limping on one leg. As I was leading prayers, I heard the voice of God's Spirit within me say that He has healed this lady and that I should tell her to start walking and throw away her crutches. I went to this lady by faith and told her what the Spirit of God had told me. She appeared frightened, looked at me and told me that the doctor had told her that she will never walk with her two legs again. She had been involved in a motor accident some years before. I told this lady, 'the greatest doctor of all time said 'He has healed you and you should start walking with both your legs.' I prayed with her, told her to believe what God had done. This lady started exercising her faith and her legs, and started walking without crutches. From that day, she never came to the church with her crutches again. This is how faith works: faith is believing and acting on what God told you every time in prayer.

A man whose son had epilepsy brought him to Jesus' disciples for healing but they couldn't heal him. The man brought this boy to Jesus and Jesus rebuked the demon, and it came out of the boy, and he was healed from that moment. Jesus' disciples asked Him why they couldn't drive out the demon, Jesus replied, *"This kind can come out only by prayer and fasting"* (Mark 9:14-29). Matthew added: *"Because you have little faith. I tell you the truth, if you have faith as small as a mustard seed, you will say to this mountain, 'move from here to there' and it will move. Nothing will be impossible for you"*

(Matthew 17:20-21). Mark revealed that the disciples of Jesus were arguing with the teachers of the law but didn't reveal their point of argument. Maybe they were arguing about the doctrine of exorcism. Whatever the point of their argument, they were unable to heal the boy.

One of the killers of faith today is people's opinion about your problems and your prayer. The disciples of Jesus have faith in God but did not have the belief that can drive out demons or heal the sick through prayer even when Jesus had given them the authority to do so. Faith that pleases God is the faith that has complete trust in God's power, words, and Spirit. It is the kind of faith that depends on God for the impossible and one that believes that everything is possible with God.

Some years ago, my wife was pregnant and was overdue to deliver. Her doctor told her that if she did not deliver the baby after two weeks, she was going to have stillbirth. She came back from the clinic and narrated the doctor's report. I encouraged her and told her that I didn't believe her doctor's report because her doctor was not the one who gave the pregnancy. We agreed to pray and fast for seven days but told her not to fast because of her condition. On the night of the seventh day of our prayer, she delivered the baby safely and healthy. This is how faith works. If we had believed the doctor's report, things might have gone wrong. Lack of faith hinders your prayers, miracles and blessing. It inspires your fears, doubt and unbelief.

7. Wrong Prayers

The most common problems that people face in prayer are the wrong prayers. Wrong prayer is asking for the wrong things. The basis of wrong prayers is wrong desire. When your desire contradicts God's desire in prayer, you pray wrongly. James the apostle declared: *"When you ask, you do not receive, because you ask with wrong motives, that you may spend what you get on your pleasures"* (James 4:3). There is nothing wrong with wanting a pleasurable life because God gives us good gifts and He wants us to enjoy them. But when what you ask in prayer takes you out of God's will or you seek pleasures at the cost of others or what you are asking for keeps you from obeying God's Word, then you are praying wrong prayers.

When you are praying that your enemies should fall and die, your prayers depends on the motive you have for your enemies, the knowledge of your enemies, and God's will for your enemies. Whatever your motives, you are praying wrong prayers because Jesus tells you in (Matthew 5:44) that you should love and pray for your enemies. When you are praying to send your wife or husband packing, you are praying wrong prayers. When selfishness and greed dominate your prayer, you are praying wrong prayers. Godly desires in prayer releases answers to prayers. Your prayer will become powerful and effective when you allow God to change your desires to correspond to His will for you.

Apostle John declared:

"Dear friends, if our heart do not condemn us, we have confidence before God and we receive from Him anything we ask, because we obey His commands and do what pleases Him."

-1 John 3:21-22

There are lots of books, tapes and teachings that inspire believers against themselves and others. The spirit of witchcraft has crept into believers' lives. When the knowledge of Satan is exalted than God's Spirit and truth, those who hold to such doctrines are locked up in the camp of Satan. They attribute everything that happened to them to Satan, evil spirit, and demons. Jesus never sent the Church to preach or teach the doctrine of Satan nor did He advise His disciples to waste their time on meaningless deliverance. Jesus sent them to go and preach the truth that will set people free from satanic lies.

In the next eight chapters, I will survey the biblical characters of men and women of God who opened heaven and manifested God's plan on earth through the power of prayer. Such giants include Moses, Joshua, Hannah, Elijah, Daniel, Jesus and the Disciples of Jesus. I will consider the common characteristics, challenges, faith, and results of their prayer life. I intend also to provoke your spirit into such a prayer lifestyle to explore the spiritual resources that God has given to you to achieve greater things in life.

POINTS ON PRAYER

- □Prayer is the licence and the authority that believers have to interfere with the supernatural.
- □You must forgive others their sin for Christ sake and for the sake of your prayers.
- □The basis of wrong prayers is wrong desire.

Chapter 4

Moses and the Power of Prayer

PRAYER IS NOT a task for lazy Christians or neutral people. It is not a matter of oratory or eloquence. It is the task of the Spirit of God and those who are filled with the Holy Spirit. The difference between Jesus' pattern of prayer and that of the disciples was the fullness of the Spirit of God in Jesus Christ. To Jesus, prayer is a lifestyle rather than a task. It is natural as well as spiritual.

There are men and women of prayer who have lived prayer lifestyles. They have used the power of prayer to change trials to testimonies, persecution to praise, languish to laughter, weeping to worship, poverty to prosperity and a horrible situation to a heavenly dwelling place. To these people, prayer is not just a task or duty; it is a communion between two spirit beings - God and man. Great men and women of God agree on a divine plan and purpose for their lives in prayer, activated by faith in the Word and the Spirit of God. To them, prayer is the master key to unlock spiritual realities, and heaven is brought to earth by their praying power. They had access to the throne of grace, interfered with natural laws and overturned demonic activities in the spirit realm.

PROPHET MOSES

Moses rose from being a shepherd to become a national prophet and a great leader in Israel. God called Moses to lead the children of Israel to the Promise Land. Moses assumed this role after much conviction to act as the Lord commanded him. Moses encountered many challenges from his congregation in their journey through the desert. At one point when Moses went to the mountain to meet the Lord, Aaron, his brother and assistant led the children of Israel astray from

God to worship a golden calf (Exodus 32:1-14). Moses stayed longer than planned on the mountain and the people of Israel had become impatient. They did not pray to inquire from the Lord what had happened to Moses but resolved to have another god instead of Moses' God. Aaron was consulted 'we need another god that will lead us. As for Moses and his God, we don't know what has happened to them.'

Aaron didn't even think about prayer; he accepted the offer of the majority and became the priest of idolatry. He invented another god for Israel to follow and worship, and sacrificed to this god. What Aaron and the children of Israel did turned their minds away from the invisible God that made Himself visible through various signs, wonders and miracles before the Israelites and the Egyptians.

Why was it that the presence of Moses was so important in the midst of the Israelites in their journey to the Promise Land? Perhaps Moses was the only figure that experienced the divine presence of God. He had heard the voice of God and seen the manifestation of God in a burning bush (Exodus 3:1-6). Perhaps Aaron and the children of Israel could not see God at work in the life of Moses. Maybe Moses was the only person that understood the need of prayer as they journeyed through the wilderness. Aaron could have chosen another way and another god, because he wanted to do things differently from the way God did things through Moses.

When a prayer lifestyle is neglected, Christians, ministers of the gospel and the entire Church could easily choose another god, another gospel or another method to worship the Living God. While Moses was on the mountain with God, Aaron was with the Israelites and was operating with the carnal counsel of the people around him. Prayer is not about bringing people's opinion to God's presence; it is affirming God's authoritative Word to the people, evidenced in authentic revelation, declaration and power.

While Moses was doing things in God's way by receiving instructions from Him on a daily basis, Aaron wanted to do things his own way and give the Israelites what they wanted. Without a prayer lifestyle, the Church is vulnerable to philosophical and popular opinion. Like Aaron, money, materialism, immorality and secular ideology could easily become another god in the Church of God.

I believe that Moses was constantly in communion with God. God said to Moses, "Look something is going in the wrong direction with the people you are leading to the Promised Land." God said:

> ***"Go down because your people, whom you brought up out of Egypt, have become corrupt. They have been quick to turn away from what I commanded them and have made themselves an idol cast in the image of a calf. They have bowed down to it and sacrificed to it and have said, these are your gods, O Israel, who brought you up out of Egypt."***
>
> ***-Exodus 32:7-8***

God was the Israelites' deliverer all along the journey from Egypt. The Israelites turned away from God's way to their own way; they were no more God's people but Moses' people. Aaron and the children of Israel only saw Moses as a great and wonderful leader with the anointing to carry out miracle, signs and wonders. They could not see the God of Israel through Moses. They could not feel the power and presence of God through him. All the miraculous deeds carried out by Moses were unable to turn them from the foreign gods of the Egyptians. Moses became 'God' to them and so it was easy for them to replace Moses when he stayed too long on the mountain.

God used the following words to describe the people He made a covenant with: 'corrupt', 'backslidden', 'idolatrous', 'hardened', and 'disobedient' all because of the popular opinion of the Israelites who had said, 'we don't know the whereabouts of Moses', and because of the failure of Aaron to approach God in prayer. If Aaron had prayed, God would have told him what was going on with Moses.

As Moses was with the Lord on the mountain, Christ the head of the Church is seated with God in heaven discussing the state of the Church, His redemptive plan and purpose, and the next task for the Church. How many popular opinions are placed before God in prayer in today's Church where politics, tribalism and personal interest have taken the role of the Holy Spirit? Philosophy and worldly wisdom are replacing the revelation of the truth of God's Word. Custom and tradition coupled with the emerging social lifestyle are adulterating sound biblical doctrines. The Church is so comfortable with praying less, choosing instead to spend time in round table meetings with a human agenda. I am not saying meetings are not important in church operations but God was not present in the meeting between Aaron and the Israelites. I also clearly declare that God is not in secular debates that sends the Spirit of God packing from some churches.

After the conclusion of their meeting, God revealed to Moses what had happened, the danger that lay ahead of them and their decision to invent another god. How did Moses react to God's anger? He used the power of prayer to switch on the heavens that were switched off by Aaron and the Israelites.

It is written 'Moses sought the favour of the Lord his God and said:

"O Lord, why should your anger burn against your people, whom you brought out of Egypt with great power and a mighty hand? Why should you let the Egyptians say, 'it was with evil intent that he brought them out to kill them in the mountains and to wipe them out off the face of the earth? Turn from your fierce anger; relent and do not bring disaster on your people. Remember your servants Abraham, Isaac and Israel, to whom you swore by your own self: 'I will make your descendants as numerous as the stars in the sky and I will give your descendants all this land I promised them, and it will be their inheritance forever. Then the Lord relented and did not bring on this people the disaster he had threatened"

-Exodus 32:11-14

Moses switched on the heavens by acknowledging the wrong doings of the Israelites. He asked God not to let the Egyptians mock His name. He stated exactly what he wanted. He reminded God about the covenant to Abraham and his descendants. While the Israelites deserved God's anger for their sins, Moses pleaded for God's mercy.

Sin is the only thing that can switch off the heavens against you. Prophet Isaiah declared; "*Surely the arm of the Lord is not too short to save, nor his ears too dull to hear. But your iniquities have separated you from your God; your sins have hidden his face from you so that he will not hear*" (Isaiah 59:1-2).

Moses realised that he needed to switch on the heavens by pleading for forgiveness and mercy on behalf of the Israelites. He was not selfish in his prayer life. He put God's people first. He stood in the gap between God and the Israelites. Moses used the power of prayer to turn off the wrath of God and to switch on the mercy and forgiveness of God for his people. You can switch off the power of God's wrath, sickness, evil, poverty, failure, disappointment, and death and switch on the power of God's forgiveness, mercy, healing, favour, blessing, riches, success, and life by the power of prayer.

Moses was both specific and direct with his request to God. He pleaded for God's mercy in place of God's anger and judgement. God made a threat that would have prompted Moses to declare himself righteous before God and made the Israelites face the consequences of their sin. However Moses realised that no one is righteous before God and that salvation from sin is an act of grace through faith. Moses put the salvation of the Israelites ahead of personal gain from God's work. This is why Jesus said,

> ***"For if you forgive men when they sin against you, your heavenly Father will also forgive you. But if you do not forgive men their sins, your Father will not forgive you your sins."***
> ***-Matthew 6:14-15***

Moses reminded God about the covenant promise of God for Abraham and his descendants in his prayer. Moses switched on the heavens by confessing the Word of God in His presence. He said to God,'*remember Abraham, Isaac and Jacob and the covenant you made with them*'.If you destroy the Israelites, you will have broken your promises for them. Moses' heaven was constantly switched on as he depended on the Word of God. In the case of the prayer Moses offered on behalf of the Israelites, he did not pray to God but prayed with God because he was in God's presence on the mountain.

Are you worried about your sin? Some people think that their sins are too many and that God cannot forgive them. God's covenant of forgiveness and restoration is available for you if you are willing to confess your sins and ask God for mercy. You too can switch on your heavens today by believing, confessing and trusting God's promises in the Bible for you. Moses did not pray out of fear of God's judgement but prayed the prayer of faith in the Word of God. You will do well in your prayer life if you can confess the promises of God for your life daily. As you believe God's Word, it will surely come to pass. The fear and feeling of your situation will never solve your problems but your faith in the Word of God and prayer will.

I was let down by someone many years ago. At the time, it appeared that I was alone in the world with no one to turn to for help. I thought there was no way out of that terrible situation; my heart was downcast. I decided to turn to God in prayer to discuss my situation with Him. I spent some days in prayer seeking for answers to my questions. During that prayer time, I had a dream that I was on a journey and was carrying a load as big as a house on my head. As I was going, I met an old man dressed in white linen with white hair and a white beard riding a golden cart. This old man asked me to put the load on my head down. I opened the big bag of load containing different items. This old man asked me to tie the entire load together and put it on his cart and sit on the cart with him to travel together to where I was going. Then I woke up from my sleep.

When I prayed over this revelation, the Spirit of God took me to 1Peter 5:7 which says: *"Cast all your anxiety on Him because He cares for you."* I meditated on this Scripture and my heart was lightened and my burdens removed! God's Spirit told me that I should never be anxious about anything in life again. He told me to commit my needs to Him in prayer all the time. You may have been in this situation before. You are like someone travelling on the bus that put his entire load on his head. You need to learn how to cast all your anxieties on God in prayer for He cares for you. There is no burden too heavy for God to carry.

Moses reacted to his difficult situation with prayer before taking action. This praying lifestyle reflected in him as a leader when the Israelites reached the Red Sea on their way to the Promised Land. When the Israelites asked Moses to show them the way forward, with the Red Sea in front of them and the Egyptian's warriors behind them, Moses did not ask or harkens to their opinion about what to do to cross over the Red Sea. Moses cried out to the Lord in prayer and God told him what to do. Moses by a miracle parted the Red Sea.

If Moses had not been around, I believe Aaron would have asked for the opinion of the Israelites elders, and said, '*What shall we do to move on men of Israel?Should we try to construct a bridge over the Red Sea or should we surrender to the Egyptian's army and go back to Egypt as slaves rather than dying in the sea?*' But Moses took the right step; he prayed, and God responded. Moses ignored the complaints and confrontation of the people, and confessed the living Word of God to their situation (Exodus 14:10-16).

-■■■■-

The power of prayer switches on your heavens; it connects you to God's revelations in dealing with your life situations. God has the right solutions to every problem. The problems you have is that most of the time, you hang between conflicting opinions - what your mind is telling you about your problems, what others tell you, and what God is saying. Moses knew that the grace of God would not take his people to where the grace of God would not provide for their needs. God told Moses, 'don't cry at the Red sea. My grace will part the sea for you'. No wonder Prophet Isaiah said:

> ***"Fear not, for I have redeemed you; I have summoned you by name; you are mine. When you pass through the waters,***

they will not sweep over you. When you pass through the rivers, they will not sweep over you. When you walk through the fire, you will not be burned; the flame will not set you ablaze. For I am the Lord, your God, the Holy One of Israel, your Saviour"

-Isaiah 43:1-3

The Word of God is loaded with solutions. You can switch on your heavens by praying the revelation of God into your situation.

Aaron's decision to worship the golden image was a big disappointment, but Moses prayed again to avert God's anger. The Lord relented from the punishment meant for the Israelites. A short and powerful prayer had saved a whole nation. Moses was not selfish in his prayer life. He could have accepted God's gracious and generous offer - 'I will make you into a great nation' (Exodus 32:10). Moses pleaded for God's mercy and God relented from His capital punishment for the sins of Aaron and Israel. Effective prayer of the righteous is still powerful and active today. Church leaders however must move from selfish service to selfless commitment to prayer to save the sinners.

Moses dealt with this national sin with God and with the Israelites. After pleading for mercy, Moses came down from the mountain and found that the children of Israel and Aaron were singing and dancing around the golden images. He destroyed the images, set them on fire and destroyed the rebellious ones. Aaron gave excuses he had feared the Israelites more than God! This is a picture of what is happening in the Church today. We pray to confess personal, communal and national sin but we don't want to deal with the sources and causes of sins. God will forgive the sins that we confess but the consequences of sins remain with us. Sin shortens life span, removes peace, aborts blessing and strains your relationship with God. He loves sinners but not their sins. If you want to be effective in your prayer life, you need to deal with your hidden sins.

Moses depended on God for all the Israelites needed to survive in order to get to the Promised Land. He confronted Pharaoh with God's help. At the Red Sea, he looked up in prayer for help. At the Desert of Sin, Moses prayed to heal bitter water when the people were thirsty. He prayed for Manna and meat when the Israelites were hungry. He also prayed for water in the wilderness and God told him to bring water out of the rock for the Israelites to drink.

Moses' prayer switched on the heavenly store house. Moses' dependence on God kept his heavens opened, empowered his intimate relationship with God, and energized his spiritual signals to hear God all the times. You too can depend on God for your daily needs. He never fails in His promises to you. If you accept Him as your creator, He has a plan for your life. You will get to know His purposes for your life each day if you can switch on your heavens through intimate relationship in prayer and study of the Word God. God has messages for you concerning your situations and problems. God is your heavenly Father with packages of good gifts. Get connected with the source of abundant blessings by switching on your prayer life.

POINTS ON PRAYER

- Prayer is not a task for lazy Christians or neutral people.
- When a prayer lifestyle is neglected, Christians could easily choose another god, gospel or method to worship the Living God.
- The power of prayer switches on your heavens and connects you to God's revelations in dealing with your life situations.

Chapter 5

Joshua and the Power of Prayer

JOSHUAISANOTHER pillar of prayer. After the death of Moses, God selected Joshua to complete the task started by Moses. God promised He would be with Joshua as He was with Moses. Joshua would be successful in leading the children of Israel to the Promised Land. At Jericho, Joshua sent men to conquer Ai but thirty six of Israel's soldiers were killed in this operation. Joshua suffered his first casualty in the assignment given to him by God. Before now the crossing of the Jordan River had taken place and the wall of Jericho had fallen. Joshua could not believe this bad news (Joshua 7:2-5). He did not call a "meeting of his Ministry of Defence." He did not question the commander of the Israel Army about the defeat. He humbled himself before God, tore his garment, fell face down before the Ark of the Lord until evening.

Joshua prayed:

"Ah Sovereign Lord, why did you ever bring this people across the Jordan to deliver us to the hands of the Amorites to destroy us? If only we had content to stay on the other side of the Jordan! O Lord what can I say, now the Israel has been routed by his enemies? The Canaanites and the other people will hear about this and they will surround us and wipe out our name from the earth. What then will you do for your own great name?"

-Joshua 7:6-9

Like Moses, the first step Joshua took was to seek God in prayer. He had learned about prayer lifestyle from Moses. He was confused and unaware of the causes of this defeat, or why the divine promise failed. Joshua wanted to know the secret to why the mighty fell, and why their military weapons had failed to win the 'Battle of Ai'. Joshua went to God in prayer until he heard God speak. Joshua knew that his spiritual warfare was not carnal but mighty in the Lord to the pulling down of strongholds (2 Corinthians 10:4). But now the stronghold of Ai had not been pulled down. He wanted to know why the power behind his victory was not at work.

Joshua needed to ask God why the divine commander of the Israel Army was absent from the battle (Joshua 5:13-15). He knew that the Israel army could not conquer without this divine commander. The military skills and intelligence had failed without the backing of God. Israel's defeat called for a divine direction that could only be ascertained by the prayer of inquiry. Joshua knew what to do - he asked God the right questions.

Pillars of prayer never accept defeat; they never give up to huge obstacles in the path of their victory. They turn mountains of problems to level ground through constant prayer. They are ready to pay the price of praying without ceasing. They spend time in dialogue with God than rather embarking on logical reasoning. Pillars of prayers don't trust their human weapons or helps; they trust the unseen hand that fights physical battles. They know that certain needs cannot be met by humans. Joshua went into God's presence to pray for Israelites' desperate needs, and God responded.

Joshua asked four key questions in his prayer: "Why this defeat?" "Why can't you allow us to settle on the other side of the Jordan?" "How can I defend this defeat with the Israelites?" and, "What will you do to give us victory and glorify your name?" Pillars of prayers don't impose their will on God, judge God from their finite knowledge, blame others for their problems or conclude from their logical reasoning. They inquire from God through constant prayer.

You may have suffered defeat in your personal life, marriage, education, business, health or spiritual battle with unseen forces, and conclude that God is not on your side. Joshua never concluded until God gave a solution to the problem of the Israelites. You may have waited in prayer to be healed from a particular sickness and given up on hope that the healing is not forthcoming but you must believe that God has not finished His work in your life yet.

Pillars of prayers don't stop praying until they receive answers to their questions. God has answers to those questions you are asking about your situation. The only way to get the answers is to switch on your heavens by offering a prayer of inquiry to God. He will respond to your questions as He did to Joshua. Stop fighting the battles of your life until you get the right message, the right weapons and the right method to fight them from God.

Charles Spurgeon said: *"Ask great things, for you are before the great throne. Oh, that we always felt this when we come before the throne of grace, for then He would do for us exceedingly abundantly above all that we ask or think." (Ephesians 3:20) (Prayer and Spiritual Warfare, page 75).*

Whenever you are in prayer, you are before the throne of grace to receive more blessings from God. Joshua knew that God was greater and more powerful than his army and their defeat. He knew the privilege of appearing in the throne of grace. He knew that he would get a solution to his defeat and so he went to God in prayer. God answered Joshua by revealing the secret for the defeat to him and what to do to gain victory. Look at God's response to Joshua's prayer:

> ***"The Lord said to Joshua 'stand up! What are you doing down on your face? Israel has sinned; they have violated my covenant, which I commanded them to keep. They have taken some of the devoted things; they have stolen, they have lied, they have put them with their own possessions. That is why Israelites cannot stand against their enemies; they turned back and run because they have been made liable to***

destruction. I will not be with you anymore unless you destroy whatever among you is devoted to destruction"

-Joshua 7:10-12

God revealed and highlighted Israel's situation to Joshua. They had sinned, broken covenant, stolen, and lied. That was the cause of their defeat. Let me ask you a logical question here: "What does military defeat has to do with stealing, breaking of covenant and telling of lies?" The heavenly army that was behind Israel victory had been offended by the action of one person among the entire nation of Israel. Sin breaks the relationship between God and His people. Sin hinders His presence, power, and provisions.

Paul the Apostle declared that *"the wages of sin is death"*(Roman 6:23).James the Apostle said that *"after desire has conceived, it gives birth to sin, when sin is fully grown, it gives birth to death"* (James 1:15). The sin of one man led to the death of 36 soldiers at a small village called Ai. One man's sin became a national plague that put Israel's security at risk. God told Joshua: "Unless you deal with this problem of sin, forget about victory in the Battle of Ai." Joshua asked God for the secret of their defeat, and he uncovered the hidden problem. Achan's sin found him out and the death penalty was the reward because he stole from "the devoted things" that God had commanded them to destroy when they conquered Jericho. This was a direct disobedience to God's command. Joshua acted on God's revelation and Achan and his family were destroyed. When the cause of sin was completely eliminated, God's presence was restored in battle. God's guidance and victory were guaranteed. God's promise of blessings was restored.

-■■■■-

Never underestimate God's Word as its consequences are severe. The only wages you receive from sin is death. Sinful actions affect others and prayers. Sin paralyses the prayer lives of believers and hinders answers from God. How sad it is that today the Church is comfortable with sin! The Church today welcome sinners with open arms, pamper them in their sin, and promise them false grace that is supposed to separate them from their sins. The Blood of Jesus and the grace of God that brings salvation is not a divinc insurance that covers a sinful lifestyle. Heaven is not promised to sinners who refuse to turn away from their wrongdoings. Heaven is for saints who repent and turn away from dead works.

How vulnerable are you to the enemy of your soul who wants you to toy with your salvation? The devil always wants you to exchange your salvation for the lust of sinful offers. How sick are you when you give in to immorality, covetousness and greed. Sin and a victorious prayer life are never compatible; salvation and sin is never a good combination.

Paul the Apostle declared that "*the grace of God that brings salvation has appeared to all men and women. It teaches us to say no to ungodliness and worldly passions and to live self-controlled, upright and godly lives in this present age*" (Titus 2:11-12). If you want to enjoy God's relationship in prayer, expect realistic results for your prayers and enjoy the fullness of God's grace in your life, you must destroy that which is devoted to destruction.

As Paul suggests; "*Put to death, therefore, whatever belongs to your earthly nature: sexual immorality, impurity, lust, evil desires and greed, which is idolatry. Because of these, the wrath of God is coming*" (Colossians 3:5-6).Joshua called for consecration and cleansing in order to win God's favour, the battle of Ai and the Promised Land. After the sin and the sinner were eradicated, God told Joshua, "Victory is yours and for your people." God said to Joshua:

> ***"Do not be afraid, do not be discouraged. Take the whole army with you, and go up and attack Ai. For I have delivered into your hands the king of Ai, his people, his city, and his land"***
>
> ***-Joshua 8:1-2***

The secret of victorious Christian living and prayer life is to expose and eradicate every hidden sin in your life, the life of your family and society. Joshua used the power of prayer to uncover the hidden troubles. He consecrated the people of God and restored God's presence and power into the scene. There is no battle that prayer cannot win if you are ready to be honest with God. He is a loving God but does not love your sinful habits. He is a merciful God but moves away from you when you cover up your secret sins. Tell Him your weakness and vulnerability. Ask for His uncommon grace to heal and cleanse you from your sins.

The hymn below gives me victory each day in my Christian Journey with Jesus:

"Be of good cheer, I have overcome the world" (John 16:33).

1. There is victory within my soul,
For the Spirit with me abides,
Let the waves of temptation roll,
Jesus keeps me whate'er betides.

Refrain:
Victory, victory, vict'ry in my soul;
I have glorious victory since Jesus took control,
Victory, victory, sweeping like a flood,
I have glorious victory through Jesus' blood.

2. Though the conflict be fierce and long,
Though the conflict my heart assail,
In my weakness yet I am strong
For with Jesus I'll e'er prevail.

Refrain

3. I have victory over sin,
I have victory o'er the grave;
Even death now has lost its sting
Hallelujah! I know I'm saved.

Refrain.

(Composed by H. Lillenas, 1885-1950).

POINTS ON PRAYER

- Pillars of prayer never accept defeat or give up to huge obstacles in the path of their victory.
- Sin paralyses the prayer lives of believers and hinders answers from God.
- The secret of victorious Christian living and prayer life is to expose and eradicate every hidden sin in your life.

Chapter 6

Hannah and the Power of Prayer

HANNAH IS ANOTHER pillar of prayer that needs to be considered. She was a married woman; a devoted woman who served God with all her heart, but she was barren. She was considered a failure and she did not have a happy marriage. Her barrenness may have been considered a cultural and social embarrassment for her husband and her family. She was subjected to reproach from her husband's second wife, Peninnah. What a horrible household! Outwardly, Hannah was considered a loser and loner; she had no child to talk to or play with. She was a woman in anguish. Peninnah's plot may have been to provoke her and push her out of the household of Elkanah. But Hannah took one major step to deal with her marital problem - she applied the power of prayer.

I remember a lady who got married some years ago in a church different to her church. I was told the pastor of her church was not happy about this and told her that she was not going to have a baby as a result of this. The woman was so concerned about his behaviour and the so - called 'prophecy' that she rang me up and we discussed the matter. I presented the living Word of God to her and encouraged her to believe in God's Word instead of the pastor's prophecy. A year later the lady rang me to share her testimony that she had delivered a baby. What a similar situation Hannah went through in her marital life.

There are thousands of believers out there who believe the prophecies of their pastors rather than the Word of God. Because of this they shipwreck their faith because they did not have the time or insight to validate such prophecies from the Scriptures. You can prove false prophecies wrong if you turn to God's Word in prayer. You must realise that not every prophecy has its origin from God's Spirit.

Apostle John declared:

"Do not believe every spirit, but test the spirits to see whether they are from God, because many false prophets have gone out into the world"

-1 John 4:1

The Scripture confirmed that Hannah wept much in the bitterness of her soul and prayed to God. And she made a vow saying,

"O Lord Almighty, if you will only look upon your servant's misery and remember me and do not forget your servant but give her a son, then I will give him to the Lord for all the days of his life, and no razor will ever be used on his head"

-1 Samuel 1:10-11

When Hannah faced ridicule, discouragement, and criticism, she brought her problems to God in prayer. She did not attribute her barrenness to Satan or to human elements. She did not pray a dangerous prayer against Peninnah. Hannah engaged God in her situation and was very positive. She had faith in God who is able to do immeasurably more than we ask or imagine according to His power that is at work in us (Ephesians 3:20). Maybe Hannah knew that God was the one who closed her womb, and that He was the only one who could open it at His own appointed time.

Hannah's faith in God was more positive than her fear of her situation. She did not spend her time fighting her husband's wife. Instead she spent quality time in prayer to God. Hannah ignored human reproach and involved God in her problem. She did not spend time in strategic warfare prayer because she knew that God was the giver of children. Her prayer was simple but powerful - she needed a son from the Lord.

Many prayers in churches today are not God centred or biblically rooted. Prayers of some men of God are culturally and traditionally motivated. Some are born out of hatred and envy. Some are carnally inclined, and some are retaliatory in nature. Prayer giants have no time to waste with satanic or demonic prayer lists. They get hold of God and the sword of the spirit to deal with their enemies. They use the creative Word of God to address what the Word of God has created. A prayer that is based on God's Word provokes God into action because He honours His Word. Prayers that engage God engage the power that created the Heavens, the earth, and the fullness therein.

In the case of Hannah, God delayed the fruit of her womb in order to display His power and glory in her life (1 Samuel 1:6, 20). Hannah's prayer however invited God into her situation. The Scripture confirmed that

"As she kept on praying to the Lord, Eli observed her mouth. Hannah was praying in her heart, and her lips were moving but her voice was not heard, Eli thought she was drunk and said to her "How long will you keep on getting drunk? Get rid of your wine." "Not so my lord, Hannah replied, I am a woman who is deeply troubled. I have not been drinking wine or beer; I was pouring out my soul to the Lord. Do not take your servant for a wicked woman; I have been praying here out of my great anguish and grief." Eli answered "go in peace, and may the God of Israel grant you what you have asked of him."

-1 Samuel 1:12-17

Hannah used the power of prayer to switch on the heaven and to call out Samuel from God.

Hannah - a woman deeply troubled

The Bible did not tell us how long Hannah was barren. She was deeply troubled because the Lord had closed her womb. Her rival provoked her in order to irritate her; her rival's words added salt to her wound. Hannah wept and would not eat at Shiloh (1 Samuel1:6). During Hannah's time, a childless woman was considered a failure. Children were a very important part of the society's economic and social structure. They were sources of blessing, help and support for the family. They cared for the parents in their old age. Hannah was troubled with what her future held for her life and marriage. She might have thought: *"Who will deliver me from this marital failure? Who will help and support me? Who will care for me when I am old? Who will inherit my portion in my husband's family?"* All these questions may have troubled her soul. Hannah was a woman who walked through the valley of barrenness; but she turned her valley of troubles into valley of blessings through prayer.

The Scripture says, *"Blessed are those whose strength is in you, who have set their hearts on pilgrimage." As they pass through the Valleys of troubles, they make it a place of springs; the autumn rains also cover it with pools. They go from strength to strength, till they appear before God in Zion.* (Psalm 84:5-7). Hannah truly appeared before God at Shiloh and she experienced the miraculous by applying the power of prayer. Hannah perceived her marital problems with the knowledge of God, as she described in her songs of praise that God was the giver of children and she prepared to meet God in prayer at Shiloh.

How you perceive your life's problems - personal, social, spiritual, marital and financial, determines how you react to such problems. You either play with your life problems or pray about them for a divine solution.

Hannah engaged in silent prayer to the Lord

Hannah knew the secret of personal and intimate prayer with the Lord. At Shiloh, Hannah moved away from partying with her family into a separate place to pour out her soul to the Lord. She didn't patch up her troubles by taking wine and beer; she didn't flow with the crowd at the conference. Hannah knew exactly what she wanted from the Lord- a son.

Jesus said, *"But when you pray, go into your room, close your door and pray to your Father, who is unseen. Then your Father, who sees what is done in secret, will reward you.* (Matthew 6:6). Hannah engaged

God in private conversation. She realised that God is the only one that could meet her needs.

Are you barren physically, matrimonially, spiritually, financially or mentally? Have you suffered grief and anguish through barrenness and still births? Are you thinking of leaving your husband or wife because you have no child? God wants you to turn your troubles over to Him in prayer. Have you been subjected to bleeding for many years and suffered a great deal from the hands of doctors and have given up hope of having a child? God is waiting to touch you at the point of your needs. You need to turn from your grief to God in prayer. He is the silent listener to every conversation and the unseen guest at every prayer meeting. Like Hannah, you can turn your heart from your crises to communion with God in prayer.

Hannah believed the Word of the Lord that came out of Eli. Hannah changed her story, her mood, her future, and her household by the power of prayer. She drew God's power of fruitfulness into her life by prayer. She silenced all her enemies, not by cursing them, but by positive and productive prayer. She turned her problems to praise by prayer and she received divine support by prayer. Pillars of prayer are those who can change time and seasons with meaningful prayer. Hannah cancelled every negative confession and assumptions by the power of prayer. You too can change your story if you are ready to apply the power of prayer to your marriage and family challenges.

God honours prayers from a sincere and devoted soul. God is a God of time and seasons. Hannah prayed but waited on God's time for her prayers to be answered. The Scripture declared:

> ***"So in the course of time Hannah conceived and gave birth to a son. She named him Samuel, saying "Because I asked the Lord for him"***
>
> ***-1 Samuel 1:20***

God's time and your time are never the same. Sarah and Abraham waited for Isaac for 25 years (Genesis 21:5), Zechariah and Elizabeth waited for God's time to have John (Luke 1:13). God is never too late.

He works out His plan in His own time. Your prayer and your patience will work together in God's agenda for your life, marriage and family. God has a set time to answer your prayers. Don't give up; your miracle is on the way.

I remember a woman who got married and had one child. She waited for seven years but did not have another. She suffered from miscarriages in all those years. She came for prayers in our church. I counselled her and asked her to believe in God, His Word and her prayers and live a sanctified live before God. God answered her prayers and she conceived and gave birth to a baby boy. This is how God answers the prayer of faith that comes from a pure heart.

POINTS ON PRAYER

- God's time and your time are never the same.
- God honours prayers from a sincere and devoted soul.
- A prayer that is based on God's Word provokes God into action because He honours His Word.

Chapter 7

Elijah and the Power of Prayer

ELIJAH IS ANOTHER prayer giant in the Scripture that we need to consider. During the time of Elijah's ministry in Israel, King Ahab and his wife Jezebel arrested and killed prophets of God. King Ahab did evil in the eyes of the Lord but not in the eyes of men. He inter-married with the Sidonians, worshiped Baal, built up altars for Baal in Israel, recruited 850 prophets of Baal and took the entire nation of Israel into the worship of other gods. Ahab also made Asherah poles to provoke God to anger. King Ahab reigned for 22 years in Israel with his throne in Samaria. Jezebel his wife was a worshipper of Baal. Both of them promoted idolatry that led Israel into sin.

Ahab and Jezebel broke the law of God given to Israel through Prophet Moses. The law says:

> ***"You shall have no other gods before me. You shall not make for yourself an idol in the form of anything, in heaven above or on the earth beneath or in the waters below. You shall not bow down to them or worship them, for I, the Lord your God, am a jealous God, punishing the children for the sin of the fathers to the third and fourth generation of those who hate me."***
>
> ***-Exodus 20:3-5***

To Ahab, Baal and Asherah poles were the same as the God of Israel; the temple of Baal was the same as the temple of the living God. Killing the prophets of God during his reign suggests that he did not want them to criticise his worship of idols, his new religion, his way of life, and his leadership. Ahab was inclusive in his religious views; he believed there was no room for criticising his new found religion. Jezebel, his wife also belonged to this religious faith.

Like the post-modern view of world religions, the greatest apostasy of this day is to place all religions on an equal pedestrian. Aggressive secularism, religious philosophies and globalisation are inventing other gods and other scriptures that are leading to new gospel, new faith and new ways of worship. If God is the same yesterday and today and forever, it is dangerous to change the truth of God's Word to suit your own selfish purposes. If the prophets of God do not rise up now, the world will soon slide into global idolatry. If men of God continue to sleep in thunder storms, the whole Earth would soon conclude that any other god is the same as the God of the Bible. That can never be true!

At that time of global idolatry and apostasy, God sent His Word through His servant, Prophet Elijah to tell Ahab the consequence of his sin against the living God. Elijah said "*As the Lord, the God of Israel lives, there will be neither dew nor rain in the next few years except at my word*"(1 King 17:1). After three years, the Word of the Lord came to Elijah: "*Go and present yourself to Ahab, and I will send rain on the land*" (1 King 18:1).

It is vital to consider the causes and consequences of sin and idolatry at this point. One man sinned; the sin spread, and the whole nation suffered the consequence. One man stood in the gap to speak to God and the nation was delivered from severe punishment. Elijah did not appear on the scene to prove himself as a powerful prophet; he was zealous for the righteousness of God. His first appearance to Ahab was to declare the Word of the Lord to the King; his second showing was to deliver God's solution and salvation to Israel.

Ahab had carried out a national pollution through his religious practices. This pollution undoubtedly called for a severe punishment. There are views that are polluting the minds of true believers today. Ahab and his subjects might have considered the punishment of God as a natural disaster of their time. They may have concluded that the only way to avert the disaster was to consult Baal for a solution.

However spiritual pollution is more dangerous than natural pollution and Baal could not help them. When the heart of man is polluted with diverse views, God gives people over to a depraved mind to do what ought not to be done. People become filled with every kind of wickedness, evil, and greed.

You need to ask a vital question here: "Where were the other prophets and priests of God who served under King Ahab?" Maybe they had been polluted by the king's religious views and had directly or indirectly supported the worship of Baal. Their voices were not heard except that of Prophet Obadiah. Obadiah was not bold enough to confront the King. He did one good job however: he supplied food to hundreds of prophets who hid themselves away from Ahab to save their life and mission. Obadiah did charitable work with a polluted mind; he was silenced by his fear of the king. You cannot compromise the truth of God's Word for charity, and you will not be saved by your good work but by your faith in God and His Word.

Prophet Elijah stood out among the prophets and priests of his time; he maintained a pure heart in the midst of polluted society. Elijah stood alone to defend the cause of the God of Israel. Prophet Elijah engaged Ahab and his 850 prophets of Baal and Asherah in sacrifice and prayer. When Ahab met Elijah, he said to him; 'You are the troubler of Israel' but Elijah told Ahab, 'You and your father's family have troubled Israel'. Elijah asked Ahab to summon all Israel and his 850 prophets of Baal to a national revival meeting at Mount Carmel. This was God's national revival through His prophet.

At the meeting, Prophet Elijah declared: *"How long will you waver between two opinions? If God is the Lord follow Him; but if Baal is God, follow him" (1King 18:21)*. But the people said nothing.

Elijah challenged Ahab, his 850 prophets of Baal and all of Israel to take a stand and follow the true God. Silence at this crucial moment could have meant that Baal and the prophets of King Ahab could be the true God because his worship and religious world view was popular among the Israelites. Silence could mean that Prophet Elijah and his God were wrong as he stood alone with the true God of Israel. But Elijah stood for God and 7000 prophets whose knees had not bowed down to Baal and whose mouths had not kissed him (1 King 19:18). Silence could imply that there were different gods of which King Ahab's god and Prophet Elijah's God were kinds. Silence could have meant that some Israelites were not sure which God was the Lord or that they knew the real God of Israel but had compromised their faith because of the sinful pleasures and other benefits that came with King Ahab's idolatrous worship.

Different religious views do not mean that there is no true God. The true God revealed himself by answering Prophet Elijah's prayer by fire. People can claim there are many gods but there is only one true God. People can claim there is no God but God is real to those who diligently seek Him in His Word and prayer. People can choose different ways of worshipping God but there is only one way of worshipping Him. Jesus has declared *"God is Spirit, and his worshipers must worship Him in Spirit and in truth" (John 4:24).*

Someone once told me that she always had problems whenever she attended church services. She said everything would go from bad to worse any time she attended church, but whenever she stopped going to church, things would get better for her. She said she believed in God, but did not believe the Bible as God's Word and that no pastor could tell her how she should live her life. Therefore she did not believe in going to church as the church told her what she should do and what she shouldn't do. This is a symptom of spiritual, moral and social decline of our time.

Andrea Minichiello William, the CEO of Christian Concern declared: "The moral and social decline in our nation is because we have turned our back on the concept of truth and God. Instead of following the Maker's instructions (His moral law) and teachings of Jesus Christ, we follow our own way and trust in our own fallen reason. Whereas society was once God-centred, now it is man-centred" (Prayer for Today, August Edition 2012, page 50). This was the state of the Israel nation under King Ahab. Prophet Elijah had to step in to reveal the true God to the Israelites. The Church will do well if they can stand up to defend the truth.

Prophet Elijah, with God's anointing engaged King Ahab and his 850 prophets of Baal in sacrifice and prayer to prove the real God to

Israel. When heaven is switched off through idolatry, atheism and secular worldview, God always has His own vessels prepared to light people's heart with the revelation of the true God. Today man-centred world is collapsing with all her wisdom and philosophy. The Church must rise up to restore the world back to God.

Prophet Elijah said *"The God who answered by fire, he is God* (1King 18:22-24). The prophets of Baal offered their sacrifice and called on their god from morning till evening but their god was silent because he was not real (1King 18:29). Prophet Elijah invited all the people and repaired the altar of the Lord, which was in ruins because King Ahab had set up another altar, another sacrifice, other prophets, another faith and another worship in Israel (1 King 19:10).

Elijah had to repair the altar of the Lord because the sacrifice that would be accepted by God must come from holy hearts and holy hands. King David declared: *"The sacrifices of God are a broken spirit; a broken and contrite heart, O God you will not despise" (Psalm 51:17).* Dead hearts, dead gods and dead worship lead to a death faith, dead church and dead society. Like Elijah, the Church needs a new heart and a renewed spirit to spark spiritual awakening in this generation. Elijah's prayer came from a pure heart, a pure spirit, and a pure passion for the presence of God. The prayer that switches on the heavens is the kind of prayer that comes from a holy heart set apart for God's use.

Prophet Elijah stepped forward and prayed:

"O Lord, God of Abraham, Isaac and Israel, let be known today that you are God in Israel and that I am your servant and have done all these things at your command. Answer me, O Lord; answer me, so these people will know that you, O Lord, are God and that you are turning their hearts back again." Then the fire of the Lord fell and burned up all the sacrifice, the wood, the stones and the soil, and also licked up the waters in the trench. When all the people saw this, they prostrated and cried, "The Lord-He is God! The Lord-He is God"

-1 King 18:36-39

The presence and prayer of Elijah did five main things in Israel. Elijah confronted King Ahab and 850 prophets of Baal and conquered them. The prophets of God who will conquer false prophets of our time, restore the nations from idolatry and evil, heal the nations from moral, social and spiritual decline are the prophets filled with the Spirit of God. The men God uses are those who are ready to work for spiritual restoration, speak only the true Word of God, preach the undiluted gospel of truth and live a holy life for the glory of God.

Elijah's prayer released the presence of God on the scene of apostasy and idolatry. The presence of God in Elijah's life brought the fire of revival to the people of Israel. Elijah caused the children of Israel acknowledge the Lord as God and agree to the eradication of Baal's prophets. He restored Israel back to God. Elijah's prayers restored rain, blessing and prosperity to the land. His prayer poured the blessing to Israel again.

The worship of God is not based on the opinion of the majority but on the revelation of the truth and the true God. The dominion of God and human knowledge are incomparable. Christ Jesus and Satan have no equal authority. The worship of nature and the worship of the creator of nature are not in any way the same. Various religious opinions may become popular but the true religion stands out. Religious worldviews and revelation of the truth have different sources and meanings. Transforming the absolute truth of the Scriptures into relative truths of philosophy are two parallel lines that can never meet. Popular opinion in the arena of revelation always blocks the mind to understanding God. You can overturn nations for the glory of God with the power of prayer.

-■■■■-

James the Apostle declared, "*Elijah was a man just like us. He prayed earnestly that it would not rain, and it did not rain on the land for three and a half years. Again he prayed, and the heavens gave rain, and the earth produced its crops. The prayer of a righteous man is powerful and effective*" (James 5:16-17). The most powerful resource you have is communication with God in prayer. How did Elijah pray? He was very serious and zealous in his prayers. He was specific in his prayer request. He prayed tirelessly without giving up hope, and one day, God told him to go and declare to Ahab what was going to happen in his time.

The amazing thing about prayer is that the result is always far greater than you can ever imagine. Elijah did not use any other weapon to defeat idolatry in Israel. He used the power of prayer to switch off the heavens and Elijah used prayer to switch it on again. You should never consider prayer as the last option when every other thing has failed. You should always consider prayer first to tap into God's power to do the unusual in your life and in the life of your community. Elijah knew that there was someone who gave rain to make crops grow and that that person was God. Elijah knew that he had access to God's presence to discuss the religious problems of his time. He was convinced that God would do something to restore his people. Elijah knew that God answers prayers. He entered into dialogue with God through prayer before he appeared to Ahab. You can change your world through the power of prayer.

POINTS ON PRAYER

- □You should never consider prayer as the last option when every other thing has failed.
- □The most powerful resource you have is communication with God in prayer.
- □God is real to those who diligently seek Him in His Word and prayer.

[illegible]

Hezpr[illegible]

to go and [illegible]

The amazing thing about prayer is that the [illegible]

[illegible]

and Elijah used [illegible]

[illegible]

Chapter 8

Daniel and the Power of Prayer

PROPHET DANIEL IS another prayer giant we need to consider. Daniel was a young slave captured by King Nebuchadnezzar who conquered Judah and took its people to Babylon. Daniel stood firm in his belief in a foreign land and he distinguished himself in his personal lifestyle, beliefs, religious views and practices. Daniel watched himself and his doctrines. Apostle Paul advises Timothy to stand firm in his daily living and in his doctrines and to persevere in order to save himself and his hearers (1 Timothy 4:16). Daniel was in a land filled with idolatrous temples and worship; he was held captive in a city where beliefs and traditions hung on astrology, enchanting, magic and sorcery.

Babylon was a nation with an image built by the king for everyone to worship. Daniel and his friends believed that God was greater and mightier than the foreign gods of Babylon. The Hebrew boys resolved not to compromise their faith during a serious crisis that could have ended their lives in an untimely manner. What power did Daniel and his friends rely on? They relied on the power of God and the power of prayer.

Let us consider what happened each time Daniel applied the power of prayer. One day, King Nebuchadnezzar had a dream he could not remember or interpret. He wanted his wise men to interpret this dream, and said that if they couldn't, they would all be killed. All the king's astrologers, sorcerers, enchanters and the magicians could not interpret the dream. The king's men had no clue and their wisdom turned into foolishness. The king ordered that all of them should be executed (Daniel 2:1-12). At this point Daniel spoke to the king's commander who was in charge of the execution and asked for permission to see the king in order to interpret the dream. Daniel left the King of Babylon and went to the King of kings in prayer to ask for interpretation to King Nebuchadnezzar's dream. The Scripture says

> ***"Daniel returned to his house and explained the matter to his friends Hananiah, Mishael and Azariah. He urged them to plead for mercy from the God of heaven concerning this misery, so that he and his friends might not be executed with the rest of the wise men of Babylon"***
>
> ***-Daniel 2:17-18***

Daniel left the king of an earth realm to meet the King of Heaven who reveals mysteries to His own, who knows everything from the beginning to the end, and who is the God who enthrones the kings of the nations. Daniel knew that when there is no solution with man, there is always a solution with God. He didn't accept the verdict of King Nebuchadnezzar because he knew that there was an ultimate verdict that prevails over every situation. The King's verdict was full of power and authority yet Daniel had the highest authority in mind. He approached the giver of human authority to nullify the authority of King Nebuchadnezzar.

Daniel knew that the prayer of the righteous is effective and powerful, and change situations for good. He realised that through prayer he would gain higher knowledge and wisdom from the highest mind. He didn't shrink in his faith in the God of Israel or allow fear of the threat of death to deconstruct his mind and reasoning. Daniel didn't seek to pray to eliminate Nebuchadnezzar so that they could be freed. He didn't enter into any *strategic* warfare prayer. He prayed the prayer of inquiry, insight and revelation into the mind of God for an answer for king Nebuchadnezzar. Daniel knew the key that unlocks the power and mysteries of God was the key of prayer.

Daniel knew that if the wise men in the service of the king couldn't help the troubled king, there is ever present help with the Living God. He knew that when human help fails, there is one help that never fails. The Psalmist declares that *"God is our refuge and strength, an ever present help in trouble"*(Psalm 46:1). There is no situation that can frighten those who know how to approach the throne of grace in times of need. God is closer to you than you think when you are in danger or crises. He is willing to listen if you can enter into a dialogue with him in prayer. Daniel prayed and God responded. The Scripture didn't tell us how long Daniel and his friends prayed for but we know that Daniel and his friends prayed to God for mercy and revelation of His mysteries. During the night the mystery of the dream was revealed to Daniel in a vision (Daniel 2:19).

What happened here? The gods of the magicians and the astrologers couldn't understand the dream and its interpretation because they were not the origin of the dream. The unfolding of the king's dream and its meaning came from God. Moses declared that "*The secret things belong to the Lord our God, but the things revealed belong to us and to our children forever, that we may follow all the words of this law" (Deuteronomy 29:29).* The power of seeing, knowing and understanding the mystery of God was given to Daniel. He prayed and God answered. This doesn't mean that Daniel was more powerful or holier than his friends; but God chose Daniel for the task and all of them enjoyed the reward of the answered prayers.

King Nebuchadnezzar promoted Daniel to a high position at the royal court after he interpreted the dream. He requested that Daniel's friends be promoted to the position of administrators in Babylon (Daniel 2:48-49). These prayer giants didn't seek for their personal interest in their prayer. Rather, they wanted an answer to a national crisis that endangered human lives. Daniel and his friends didn't place themselves above the king of Babylon. All they sought for was to prove the power and presence of God.

Panic in the face of crises cripples your faith, hope and trust in the power of God. Rather than bowing down for the king's verdict, Daniel and his friends chose God's power over panic. While panic was marching the king's wise men to their graves, God's power propelled Daniel and his friends to the realm of life givers and life savers. These men were convinced that they could save lives through the power of prayer.

The power of God's wisdom and revelation is the key that opens the door out of crises. Crises always cringe in the presence of Christ Jesus our Lord. When Daniel received the answer to his prayer, he praised God that revealed that mystery. Daniel praised God of heaven and said:

> ***"Praise to the name of God forever and ever; wisdom and power are his. He changes times and seasons; He sets up kings and deposes them. He gives wisdom to the wise and knowledge to the discerning. He reveals deep and hidden things; He knows what lies in darkness, and light dwells with him. I thank and praise you, O God of my fathers: You have given me wisdom and power, you have made known to me what we ask of you, and you have made known to us the dream of the king"***
>
> ***-Daniel 2:20-23***

I want you to note the phrases 'He changes', 'He sets', 'He gives', 'He reveals', 'He knows', and 'You have given...' Daniel knew his God intimately and knew that He is the giver of all things. God is in charge of the world affairs and all of our lives. He is the power behind every kingdom. Nothing happens without his fore-knowledge. You can tap into the mystery of the future through prayers of inquiry. The problem we face today however is that we usually accept that whatever is happening is normal. We fail to approach God for the secrets behind events. Daniel used the power of prayer to prevail over the king's verdict. You can change the world for God through his Word and prayer. With the presence of God in your life, you can reign and shine in the midst of darkness.

The power of prayer was not done in Daniel's life. Nebuchadnezzar had another dream in his palace. Despite the miraculous interpretation of the first dream, the king didn't give up the worship of idols. Nebuchadnezzar was contented and prosperous. He placed himself at the top of the world affairs. His comment to Daniel shows that the king believed in many gods. He told Daniel 'surely your God is the God of gods and the Lord of the kings and the revealer of mysteries, for you were able to reveal this mystery.' The making of a golden image perhaps was to put the God of Daniel under the control of the gods of Babylon where Nebuchadnezzar was king. Although Nebuchadnezzar praised Daniel's God for His wonders, he didn't believe in Him completely or submit to His authority (Daniel 4:1-3, 8). Nebuchadnezzar believed in the names and spirit of the gods of his land. What a confession without possession of God!

Confessing God is not the same thing as obeying Him. While Daniel revealed the future plan of Nebuchadnezzar's kingdom to him, he still insisted on do things in his own way.

-OOOO-

The danger facing the 21st Century Church is confession without possession of God's presence and revelation of His will. We confess Jesus Christ as Lord and head of the Church but His Word and His will are not the forces guiding the Church. We confess that God is holy but we assume that every other god is equal to the living God. We confess that we have fellowship with Him yet we are consumed with greed, selfishness and immorality. We confess that He is in control of our lives and the Church's affairs yet we have idols stationed all around in the Church. The different portrait of God being painted by the so called pastors shows that their belly is their God.

According to Apostle Paul,

"Many live as the enemies of the Cross of Christ. Their destiny is destruction, their god is their stomach, and their glory is in their shame. Their mind is on earthly things"

-Philippians 3:18-19

God knew that Nebuchadnezzar's heart had not changed. Nebuchadnezzar only worshiped the God of Daniel with his mouth but his heart was far from Him. The God of Daniel gave another dream that Nebuchadnezzar could not interpret regarding his future and the future of his kingdom. Sometimes your heart may be carried away from God's plans for you due to the contentment and prosperity you enjoy presently. The gods of money and materialism is taking their toll in the heart of today's Christians. The message of salvation and holiness is suffering at the expense of secular gospel.

There is no adjective that can be used to describe the gospel that Jesus preached and the gospel He sent His disciples to preach to the world. Jesus' gospel is directly revealed from the living God as contained in His living Word. Any other gospel preached today is the product of human philosophy. While Nebuchadnezzar preached his own gospel through golden images, the God of Daniel revealed his authentic message through interpretations given to his servant Daniel.

Nebuchadnezzar invited Daniel to interpret his dream because he believed that the spirit of the 'holy gods' was in Daniel. The king had misunderstood the Spirit of God in Daniel as the Spirit of 'the gods'. The king, the wise men, the astrologers, the magicians and the enchanters knew that there was a different spirit in Daniel which gave him the ability to interpret dreams, but they didn't know the giver of that spirit. The Spirit of God in Daniel endowed him with God's ability to serve and be promoted in Babylon. By the Spirit of God, Daniel told the king the meaning of his dream that would lead to the end of Nebuchadnezzar's kingdom. God humbled Nebuchadnezzar and made it clear who was the true God. What an excellent Spirit that lived in Daniel? This Spirit searches all things, even the deep things of God. Jesus Christ, for this reason told His disciples to wait for the Holy Spirit before they started on their mission to evangelise the world.

Those who are led by the Spirit of God are the children of God. The power of prayer and revelation is given by God's Spirit. Nebuchadnezzar learned his lessons the hard way; he later accepted that the Most High was in control of the world and human affairs. At the end of his insanity, Nebuchadnezzar confessed that God is the one that lives forever; that He has eternal dominion, everlasting kingdom, sovereign choices, dominion over all peoples, power over all powers, and that I the King of heaven, does what is right and His ways are just (Daniel 4:34-36).

Daniel used the power of prayer in a dynamic way while he was in exile. When Darius discovered the divine skills and gifts in Daniel, and how God had used him to interpret the hand writing on the wall, the king appointed Daniel as one of the administrators over the provincial governors. There was a conspiracy to eliminate Daniel from this position by the enacting of a decree that no one should pray for 30 days. Anyone that disobeyed the king's decree was to be killed by being thrown into a Lion's den. The conspirators knew that there was no other way to capture Daniel except through his commitment to prayer. Daniel had already proven himself as a man of noble character, a person with sound principles and a servant with exceptional qualities. When Daniel heard that the decree had been signed into law, he went upstairs in his room and opened the windows towards Jerusalem. Daniel got down on his knees and prayed three times a day, giving thanks to God, as he had done before (Daniel 6:1-10).

Daniel had a prayer room in his house. There was no temple for the Jews in Babylon and the king wanted the people to worship the gods of the land. The only place of worship therefore was the temple of the gods of Babylon. Daniel turned his house to a prayer centre. He knew that the strategy of the devil and his conspirators was to stop him for praying to his heavenly Father. Today, the devil is hunting down many people's prayer lives through diverse systems - post modernism, religiousness and secularism. Believers today can spend hours with movies, fun, sports, talks and gossip that take them away from prayer and the study of the Word of God.

How often we give up defeating of the enemies, for fear of persecution, and careless compromise because we cannot spend our time in prayer. Daniel knew that for him not to pray for 30 days would cause him to spend his prayer time for something worthless. He refused to let his conspirators stop him from praying three times a day. He knew that the secret of his success, promotion, protection and favour among the rulers of Babylon was not his power but the power of the Almighty God. One hundred and twenty men stood against Daniel to pull him down the ladder of God's plan for him but they did not succeed because God stood by him.

Post-modern Christians and Prayer

Prayer life in the Church is under pressure as post-modern Christianity is battling with advanced philosophy, science and popular world views. I have heard some Christians say, "How can you pray for hours? What exactly are you asking for?" I have heard theologians argue that any prayer outside the 'Lord's Prayer' recorded in Matthew 6:9-13 is unbiblical. There are conflicting views about prayer which have watered down the power of prayer in the post-modern Church. I think we need to ask Daniel 'What were you praying for three times a day?' and he would tell you: 'I have battles to win; I have lions' teeth and tearing power to silence; I have dreams to interpret; I have visions to fulfil; I have a future to know about; I have good news to share with the next generations."

Daniel wouldn't stop there; he would add: I have praise to offer to God. I have an assignment to complete in the king's palace; I have a revelation to receive from the Most High; I have petitions to make for my family, friends and the nation of Israel; I have the word of the prophets to read and understand; the future is both great and challenging; I cannot afford to play with my destiny." With all these tasks, Daniel could not play with his prayer time.

The Church of today is drifting away from their primary task to baseless arguments that won't change the world for God's glory. The Apostles of Jesus also discovered the secret of the power of prayer; they concluded that they must give their attention to prayer and the ministry of the Word (Acts 6:4).

Daniel did not give all his attention to the king's service or the noise of his conspirators; he focused on prevailing prayer in his house. His conspirators found Daniel praying and asking God for help (Daniel 6:11). He was taken from his prayer room to the Lion's den. Daniel did not lobby the king for help; he did not go to the palace to defend himself. Rather, he ignored his conspirators; he dismissed the law issued against his prayer life, and engaged the One who is able to suspend the laws of nature. Daniel knew that the king, the law, the conspirators and the lions were subject to the Almighty God.

The Scripture is not clear what Daniel's prayer points were, but I perceive that Daniel prayed for divine intervention. There was no way Daniel could have handled the case set against him without help from above. While Daniel's conspirators were plotting to find fault and accuse him of violating the law of the Medes, he found faith in God to fault his conspirators. The king gave in to the conspirator's report that Daniel had disobeyed the decree of the King, and Daniel was thrown into the lions' den.

The king remarked that Daniel was a faithful child of God and said *'May your God, whom you serve continually rescue you'* (Daniel 6:16). The king knew that Daniel served a God that was different from their gods. The king also called Daniel 'servant of the living God' the second day he was thrown into the den (Daniel 6:20). Daniel did not fear the lions but fanned the flame of the Spirit of God in him. He also fired his faith by the past testimonies he had had with God. Daniel took time to pray before going to the lions' den. His praise and prayer signalled his belief in how God was going to rescue him from the hand of his conspirators.

Prayer is not a casual spiritual exercise; it is an act of intimacy. Most Christians pray when they are in the den of problems; they fail to pray ahead in order to tap into spiritual realities. When the king put Daniel into the Lions' den, his response showed that he did not hate the king for signing the decree. He knew there was a greater King who could overrule the consequence of the law. Daniel said:

> ***"O king, live forever! My God sent his angel, and shut the mouths of the lions. They have not hurt me because I was found innocent in his sight. Nor have I ever done anything wrong before you O king"***
>
> ***-Daniel 6:21-22***

Daniel's prayer sent angels ahead of him to the lions' den and shut the mouth of the beasts. His prayer brought him out of the lions' den because he trusted his God and no wound was found on him. The scripture reveals that '*through faith the prophets conquered kingdoms, administered justice, and gained what was promised; who shut the mouths of lions, quenched the fury of the flames and escaped the edge of the sword*'(Hebrew 11:33-34). Daniel ranked among men of great faith in the scripture; he stood alone with God in the face of persecution. You can conquer kingdoms, administer justice, gain God's promises for your life, shut the mouth of the wicked ones, quench the fury fire of the enemies and escape deadly sickness by the power of prayer.

You need to consider the testimony of Daniel to the king. Daniel affirmed that he had done nothing wrong before the king and the law of the land. His conspirators and the decree issued against his prayer life that were the problem. Daniel knew the law was enacted to destroy his faith and prayer life. He affirmed that he was innocent in the sight of God even though his enemies thought he was wrong for disobeying the decree. Sometimes, what is wrong in the sight of man is not wrong in the sight of God. What seems right in the sight of God may sometimes be seen as wrong by men. Daniel's faith did not hang on what was going on around him but on the living God and His eternal power. He was a praying saint and not a praying sinner. Daniel was not a criminal Christian; he trusted God and prayed, and God delivered him from a horrible death.

-■■■■-

Jesus said '*blessed are the pure in heart for they will see God*' (Matthew 5:8). David said '*if I had cherished sin in my heart the Lord would not have listened to me*' (Psalm 66:18).The true winners in God are those who win the battle of sin, Satan and the flesh. You too can win your battle by prayer and faith in God. You can shut the mouth of the enemies that are roaring like lions seeking to devour you and your destiny. You can overcome all your life battles through the power of prayer. You can switch off the evil thoughts against you if you switch on the heavens with prayer.

POINTS ON PRAYER

□Prayer is not a casual spiritual exercise; it is an act of intimacy with God.

□The power of God's wisdom and revelation is the key that opens the door out of crises.

□The prayer of the righteous is effective and powerful, and change situations for good.

○

Chapter 9

Daniel and the Power of Prayer II

DANIEL ALSO USED the power of prayer to affect the destiny of the entire nation of Israel in captivity. He understood from the Word of God through Prophet Jeremiah that the desolation of Jerusalem would last for 70 years (Daniel 9:2). He had insight into the events, the time, and the seasons. Daniel did not start praying at the middle of this specified period but at the completion of the time declared by God through His servant. Daniel knew that the time of returning and restoration had come for Israel and he approached God in His Word and prayers.

Daniel's prayer life was not based on his feelings, the political agenda of his days, or fear of the unknown. Daniel knew where to meet God and where God inhabited. He knew that God would never act contrary to His decreed Word. There is revelation for every situation! What the 'Ancient of Days' had decreed regarding individuals, families, societies, nations, and the second coming of the Lord Jesus Christ will surely come to pass. What God has said is vital to what He will do. Every challenge you face is temporary; only God is eternal and everlasting. While other Jews gave up hope in captivity, Daniel searched for God's plan and the promises in the scriptures. He believed what God said and prayed them out in faith.

Daniel turned to the Lord in prayer, petition and fasting. He prayed to the Lord his God and confessed:

> ***"Lord, the great and awesome God, who keeps his covenant of love with those who love him and keep his commandments, we have sinned and done wrong. We have been wicked and have rebelled; we have turned away from your commands and laws. We have not listened to your servants the prophets, who spoke in your name to our kings, our princes and our***

ancestors, and to all the people of the land. Lord, you are righteous, but this day we are covered with shame—the people of Judah and the inhabitants of Jerusalem and all Israel, both near and far, in all the countries where you have scattered us because of our unfaithfulness to you. We and our kings, our princes and our ancestors are covered with shame, Lord, because we have sinned against you. The Lord our God is merciful and forgiving, even though we have rebelled against him; we have not obeyed the Lord our God or kept the laws he gave us through his servants the prophets. All Israel has transgressed your law and turned away, refusing to obey you.

Therefore the curses and sworn judgments written in the Law of Moses, the servant of God, have been poured out on us, because we have sinned against you. You have fulfilled the words spoken against us and against our rulers by bringing on us great disaster. Under the whole heaven nothing has ever been done like what has been done to Jerusalem. Just as it is written in the Law of Moses, all this disaster has come on us, yet we have not sought the favour of the Lord our God by turning from our sins and giving attention to your truth. The Lord did not hesitate to bring the disaster on us, for the Lord our God is righteous in everything he does; yet we have not obeyed him.

Now, Lord our God, who brought your people out of Egypt with a mighty hand and who made for yourself a name that endures to this day, we have sinned, we have done wrong. Lord, in keeping with all your righteous acts, turn away your anger and your wrath from Jerusalem, your city, your holy hill. Our sins and the iniquities of our ancestors have made Jerusalem and your people an object of scorn to all those around us. Now, our God, hear the prayers and petitions of your servant. For your sake, Lord, look with favour on your desolate sanctuary. Give ear, our God, and hear; open your eyes and see the desolation of the city that bears your Name. We do not make requests of you because we are righteous, but because of your great mercy. Lord, listen! Lord, forgive! Lord, hear and act! For your sake, my God, do not delay, because your city and your people bear your Name."

-Daniel 9:4-19

THE ATTRIBUTES OF DANIEL'S PRAYERS

1. Awareness of God's Covenant of Love

Daniel started his prayer by declaring God's greatness, awesomeness, andfaithfulness to His covenant of love. He knew that God disciplines in love. He praised God for who He is, the covenant He made with Israel and His faithfulness to this covenant. Daniel realised that God is just and faithful in dealing with His people. He praised God who forgives, forgets and restores people from their sins with love. Daniel knew how to approach God in prayer. He switched on the heavens by praise.

How do you react when you face life's problems – whether test of faith, troubles, and domestic challenges, financial down turn, loss of job, marriage break down or loneliness? Do you remember God's covenant of love for you and His great power over your situation? The key that unlocks your heavens in prayer no matter your situation is realising that God's covenant of love is with you. He has promised that He will be with you always (Matthew 28:20). You don't judge God with your finite mind as His thoughts and ways are higher than yours and unsearchable. When you think that God is angry with you, He is happy and loves you. His love is eternal and everlasting. Even when relatives and friends forsake you, God will never break His covenant of love with you until you break away from Him. If you are willing to turn to God today, He will receive you with open arms.

2. Awareness of God's Righteousness and Truth

Daniel knew that God was righteous and true in His judgement. He accepted God's judgement for Israel nation caused by their disobedience to God's commandments. He knew that God was right to correct His people when they acted unfaithfully. Daniel knew that Israel had broken the terms of God's covenant as stated in the scripture and as taught by their prophets. Daniel knew that God could never be wrong in punishing His people for their wrong doing. God is righteous and true to His Word. His golden rules for living are clearly stated in the Scripture for you. Breaking such rules attract God's punishment.

You cannot hide your unrighteous act from God's presence. He is the all-knowing God. Breaking the rules of God can switch off your heavens as God has no relationship with an unholy heart, life or worship. You cannot access God's righteousness and truth with your feeble mind or philosophy. You cannot decide on God's behalf what is right or wrong. You cannot worship God in your own way as He has established His standard for you in His Word. Acknowledging your wrongdoing when you are praying is vital to attracting God's forgiveness and favour.

Jesus declared, *"For I tell you that unless your righteousness surpasses that of the Pharisees and the teachers of the law, you will certainly not enter the kingdom of heaven"* (Matthew 5:20).

True righteousness with God is one that flows from a changed heart and attitude. This is the kind of righteousness that switches on your heavens. When you are in prayer, be sincere and honest with yourself. God already knows what is in your heart. Don't cover up your sins. He knows every secret of your heart. God doesn't need a lie detector to uncover your deceptions. He is the creator of your heart and He knows the good and bad thoughts that come out of it all the time.

3. Awareness and expression of God's Attributes

Daniel declared God's attributes in his prayer. He knew that God is a loving and merciful God, who corrects and rebukes in love. Daniel realised that God's love and mercy are eternal and everlasting for His people. Daniel realised that the reason why they were in their mess was because Israel had rebelled against God and His laws. They switched off the love, mercy and blessings of God and switched on curses upon themselves (Deuteronomy 28). God's terms were clear: obey God and enjoy His full blessings, or disobey God and experience His full wrath.

If God's love and mercy are eternal and everlasting, His anger, judgement and wrath are eternal as well. God will remain faithful to His Word and He will never change. You may get away with breaking civil law but you cannot get away with breaking the Word of God. He has demonstrated His love to the world by sending His son to die for our sins. John declared, *"Whoever believes in the Son has eternal life, but whoever rejects the Son will not see life, for God's wrath remains on him"* (John 3:36). The only way to enjoy the presence of God is to obey God and His Words and put them into practice. You will win God's favour and human favour daily and you can hear Him speaking to you on a daily basis. You will experience uncommon peace and enjoy unbroken relationships and communion with Him.

4. Awareness of Israel's wrongdoing

Daniel acknowledged the wrongdoing of Israel in his prayer. He said 'we have sinned and done wrong', 'we have been wicked and have rebelled', 'we have turned away from your commands and laws', 'we have not listened to your servants the prophets', Daniel did not blame others for their problems. Daniel assessed their problems from the Word of God, their relationship with God and their way of worship. Daniel looked at the inner hearts of his people and their attitude towards God's law. He realised that there was rebellion, wickedness, disobedience in their hearts. Daniel realised that sin was what had switched off their heavens and meted God's punishment on them.

Sin is also the main obstacle to your prayer life. You must search your heart to know how you think about God, your problems and people around you. Sin always has its root in thoughts and as Jesus declared; *"For from within, out of men's hearts, come evil thoughts, sexual immorality, theft, murder, adultery, greed, malice, deceit, lewdness, envy, slander, arrogance and folly. All these evils come from the inside and make a man unclean"* (Mark 7:21-23). These sins disconnect your heart from God's Spirit and His Word. You need to examine your inner heart whenever you are in prayer with God, confess your sins and ask for forgiveness. I have heard of some Christians say they cannot forgive others their sins because of their evil deeds. But Jesus said*'If you do not forgive men their sins, your Father in heaven will not forgive you your sins'* (Matthew 6:15). Search your heart before you search for God in prayer because your heart is God's temple.

5. Awareness of God's Punishment for Sin

Daniel affirmed that his people deserved what they got. Daniel acknowledged, *'we are in captivity, scattered all over the place because of our unfaithfulness to you'*. God is a loving God who bases His judgement on the laws given to His people. Daniel expressed the attitudes and qualities of a true praying heart. He surrendered completely to God, expressed complete openness, honesty and humility in expressing the sins of Israel and in accepting their faults and the punishment received. He did not accuse God as some Christians do in their feeble judgements. It takes faith and obedience of God's Word to accept suffering, sickness, famine, crime and death as punishment for sin; and that true repentance, confession and turning to God lead to complete healing and restoration.

Every wrongdoing has a consequence on your physical, spiritual, social and moral life. When your heaven is switched off through sins, you are in the territory of the devil. You can be tormented and afflicted by evil forces. You need to reconnect yourself with God through His Word and prayer to release yourself from the devil. No amount of deliverance prayers can save a sinner who remains in sin. The first step of recovery from bondage is genuine repentance and faith in the redemptive work of Jesus Christ and the Word of God. Daniel realised this truth and he spent time in prayer to explore the sins and judgement of Israel from the Word of God. You can set yourself free from God's punishment by repenting and turning from your sins today.

6. Awareness and Affirming the Infallibility of God's Word

Daniel declared, "You have fulfilled the Words spoken against us and against our rulers by bringing on us great disaster." Daniel understood that God never makes mistake with what He has said. His 'yes' means 'yes' and 'no' means 'no'. The 'do' and 'don't' of God can never change. Whatever God said in His Word will be fulfilled in His own time. The world and people in it may change, and people may mis-interpret the Word of God to suit their purposes but God will never change His written and revealed Words.

Jesus declared, *"Do not think that I have come to abolish the Law or the Prophets; I have not come to abolish them but to fulfil them. I tell you the truth, until heaven and earth disappear, not the smallest letter, not the least stroke of a pen, will by any means disappear from the Law until everything is accomplished"*(Matthew 5:17-18). God fulfils His Word in two ways: He blesses when you obey and do His will and punishes when you disobey and forsake His will. The laws of God are so active; when you disobey them, you suffer the consequences even after you repented from your sins. The laws of God place you under closed or open heaven depending on your obedience or disobedience. Never take God for granted as what He said is binding. Don't play with the curses and blessings written in the Word of God; they are spirit and life (John 6:63). As the Word of God blesses, it also burns as a consuming fire.

7. Awareness and Acknowledging Past Miracles of God

Daniel acknowledged the past miracles of God with His people; how He delivered their forefathers from Egypt with His mighty hands and defeated their enemies in the Red Sea. Daniel realised that if God did such miracles in the past, God could still do it in his own time and even now. Daniel believed that their freedom, restoration and blessings were packaged in God's power. This conviction motivated him into prayer.

Whatever your problems, your faith in the miraculous power of

God is sufficient to help you out. This is why Jesus was anointed by the Holy Spirit to preach the good news to the poor, to proclaim freedom for the prisoners and recovery of sight for the blind, to release the oppressed, and to proclaim the year of the Lord's favour (Luke 4:18-19). Your faith in Jesus Christ places you in the realm of God's miraculous power, switches on your miraculous heavens, connects you with the ultimate power that can do all things, and liberate you from unseen forces of darkness. Your faith in God gives you licence to tap into the fullness of God's power to dismantle every network of evil that enslaves your soul. This power is at work in your heart when you receive the baptism of the Holy Spirit. This power is also able to do immeasurably more than all you ask or imagine in your prayer. Your faith in God and His miraculous power helps you to unseat the devil and his works. You can level your mountains with faith.

8. Awareness of Specific Prayer Request

Daniel was clear and specific in his prayer request for his people. He asked God to turn away His anger and wrath from Jerusalem, the city of God. He asked for forgiveness and for God's favour on the sanctuary of God and his people. Daniel searched his prayer requests from the scriptures. He did not base his prayer requests on his own feelings or pressure from Babylon. Daniel did not outline dangerous prayer requests for his enemies or the enemies of Israel. He allowed the Word of God and the Spirit of God to guide his prayer requests. Daniel knew what to pray for because he traced their problems to the Word of God.

Most prayers today are not rooted in the scriptures. Prayers today are motivated by hatred, tradition, selfishness, greediness, covetousness, pride, demonic awareness and fear. Most prayers are personal reasons and not for others.

How do you assess your prayer requests in the Word of God? What motivates you into prayer and fasting? Is it because you want your enemies to die or you want the whole world to be yours? Stop wasting your time and energy in such prayers. They are not godly or biblical.

Search the scriptures for whatever you want to pray about and make sure that it aligns with God's Word and God's will and you will surely receive answers to your prayer. Learn to pray a few godly prayers than many ungodly prayers.

9. Awareness of God's Act for His own Name

Daniel asked God to hear his prayers for God's own sake and not for Daniel or Israel's sake. Daniel asked God to respond to his prayers according to God's will, favour and mercy. Daniel was not forcing his prayers or imposing his will on God. He asked God to bless His people again, keep his people from shame and make His face shine upon Israel. Daniel asked God to be gracious to the people, to turn His face towards Israel and give them peace by bringing them to their land of promise. Daniel asked God for the blessings of restoration and renewal of a covenant of peace with His people. Daniel's prayers and petitions were not based on his own or Israel's righteousness but on God's righteousness, favour, mercy, love, and promises. God honours prayers from a humble, honest, open and surrendered heart and He answered Daniel.

10. Awareness of God's Identity with His People

Daniel prayed and said, *"Give ear, O God, and hear; open your eyes and see the desolation of the city that bears your Name. We do not make requests of you because we are righteous, but because of your great mercy. O Lord, listen! O Lord forgive! O Lord, hear and act! For your sake, O my God, do not delay, because your city and your people bear your Name"* (Daniel 9:18-19).

While the Israelites may wonder why the city and temple of God were destroyed with its inhabitants scattered by the Babylonians, Daniel realised from the prophecy of Jeremiah that the temple, the city and the people of God were not automatically protected from God's punishment if they sinned and violated the laws and commandments of God. The name of God symbolised the presence and act of God in the temple, where God met with His people and where people met their God in prayer.

Daniel saw this truth in the book of Jeremiah as God told Jeremiah:

"Go now to the place in Shiloh where I first made a dwelling for my Name, and see what I did to it because of the wickedness of my people Israel. While you were doing all these things, declares the Lord, I spoke to you again and again, but you did not listen; I called you, but you did not answer. Therefore, what I did to Shiloh I will now do to the house that bears my Name, the temple you trust in, the place I gave to you and your ancestors. I will thrust you from my presence, just as I did all your fellow Israelites, the people of Ephraim.'

So do not pray for this people nor offer any plea or petition for them; do not plead with me, for I will not listen to you. Do you not see what they are doing in the towns of Judah and in the streets of Jerusalem? The children gather wood, the fathers light the fire and the women knead the dough and make cakes to offer to the Queen of Heaven. They pour out drink offerings to other gods to arouse my anger. But am I not the one they are provoking declares the Lord? Are they not rather harming themselves, to their own shame? Therefore this is what the Sovereign Lord says: My anger and my wrath will be poured out on this place—on man and beast, on the trees of the field and on the crops of your land—and it will burn and not be quenched"

-Jeremiah 7:12-20).

God was the one who initiated the place of worship (Shiloh and the Temple) in Jerusalem; the mode, terms and conditions of worship. He also made a covenant to answer their prayers whenever they called upon Him. However, the holiness of God cannot relate to the ungodliness of man. Daniel concluded his prayers by calling for the restoration of His divine presence in the heart of the Israel nation. It was the sins of Israel people that removed God's presence from them. The scripture declares that '*you are the temple of God and the Spirit of God lives in you*' (1 Corinthian 3:16). You cannot claim that you have the Spirit of God in you if sins control your life. Those sins that destroy your temple - sexual immorality, impurity, lust, evil desires, greed, anger, rage, malice, slander, envy, hatred and filthy languages must be removed before you can connect to the presence, peace and power of God.

God's laws were given to help people love and worship God with all their hearts and minds. During the time of Daniel and Jesus, Israel abused the laws of God, misinterpreted and misapplied it to suit their own ways. The religious, civil and moral laws and the Ten Commandments are still valid to God and His people today. The consequence of obeying or disobeying the laws of God cannot be changed.

It is essential for you to appreciate how Daniel put Israel's problem of desolation and captivity in perspective. In his view, Israel was not a victim of war between Babylon and Israel. It was not the case of lack of sophisticated weapons and men of valour. It was not a matter of the Devil or evil spirit that calls for strategic territorial warfare prayers. The Israelites had suffered defeat and gone into captivity because of their disobedience and rebellion against the Word of God. The suffering of Israel in a foreign land had resulted from neglecting God's divine law which form the basis of the covenant relationship with His people. Captivity was therefore a punishment from the Lord.

Some Israelites in captivity could have thought that God was wicked to them or that their leaders were too weak to defeat an external attack. Some might even have thought that the idea of God was fake or a myth. Whatever their views, Daniel's views were right and biblically sound. He knew that criticism or conflicting political and religious views would not set the Israelites free from captivity. Daniel knew that the solutions necessary were the knowledge of God and His Word, repent once and prayer for forgiveness and mercy.

Apostle Paul declared that *'disobedience is a spirit that is at work in the heart of those who choose to fall away from the will of God'* (Ephesians 2:1-2). Unfaithfulness, rebellion, and rejecting God and

His Word breaks God's covenant. As is the case today, the Israelites ignored the Word of God through the prophets, regarding them as mere products of human instinct. The prophets informed them about the punishment that would result from their rebellion. The truths spoken by the prophets were too painful to hear; their preaching was too hard to follow; and their teachings were considered a breach of their human rights. At that time of spiritual backsliding in Israel, false prophets declared what the people wanted to hear. God's voice in a rebellious world sounds like foolishness to those who hear them. But Daniel believed that the word of the true prophets came directly from God and that it will be fulfilled.

Daniel knew who to turn to during a national calamity and disaster. The king, the wise men, the Levites and the entire Israelites may have lost hope during the 70 years of captivity. Some of their loved ones would have died. The rest were probably immigrant slaves who had no rights and entitlements to the citizenship of Babylon. The people left behind could do nothing than to give up and accept their situation as normal. Daniel was determined to seek the face of God and His future plans for his people. Daniel's determination showed the love he had for his people. He was not selfish in his prayers.

Daniel could have been complacent because of his achievements in Babylon, but he was not satisfied with the king's promotion and titles. Daniel discovered that there was no situation too difficult for God to address. He turned to search for God in His Word and he interceded for Israel's spiritual and religious restoration. You can change your life, marriage, family, community, nation and the world through prayer.

Daniel's prayers can be divided into four sections:

1. Prayer of Praise (Daniel 9: 4, 7)

Daniel praised God for His greatness, awesomeness, faithfulness, love, righteousness and truthfulness. His perspective of God's nature and aracter towards His creation was absolutely credible. Daniel saw od as the right judge and decision maker, who based His justice and dgement on the law given to Moses. Daniel saw God as the one in arge of creation, all human affairs, and the Israel nation. He knew at God is a Father, who disciplines his loved ones when they do ong. The scripture records that *'My son, do not make light of the rd's discipline and do not lose heart when he rebukes you because e Lord disciplines those he loves, and he punishes everyone he cepts as a son'*(Hebrew 12:5-6*)*. God's greatness, faithfulness and e were displayed in creation and He sustained what He created h His powerful Word. God's law was not meant to restrict Israel's itical, social, economic, spiritual or religious freedom; it was put place to boost the relationship between God and man in order to oy what God has freely given.

Daniel did not fail to praise God for fulfilling His incarnate Word ustice and love. He knew that God's judgement was full of favour l mercy. He knew that God would not discipline to destroy but to ld up His people in the knowledge of His character and being. enever God disciplines, He is willing to restore you back to the ginal mutual relationship. Daniel praised God because he knew t His love and favour towards His covenant people was greater n His punishment. He is a God who rebukes, restores, reveals and ards His people at His own appointed time.

Prayer of Petition (Daniel 9: 5-6)

iel did not declare himself righteous when he turned to God in ver. He identified himself with the national sin of disobedience rebellion. Daniel stated clearly: '*We have sinned and done wrong, have been wicked and have rebelled; we have turned away from r commands and laws; we have not listened to your servants the phets, who spoke in your name to our kings, and our princess'* niel 9:5-6). Daniel knew from the Scripture that doing what is itually and morally wrong is sin against God. He knew that turning the law of God to suit our natural purpose was acting in error. He knew that confronting the word of the Prophets who declared the counsel of God was rebellion. He went to the root of the problem of Israel's punishment, shame and curse. He outlined the nation's sins before God, and prayed for God's forgiveness and mercy.

The problem of evil in today's world is a subject of intense debate among the Christian and secular philosophers. Some consider evil as a natural phenomenon, while some trace evil to the Devil and the fallen angels. However, what you may fail to consider is the link between the creator, the creation and the work of restoration with the Word of the creator. The creator puts the creation under subjective rules and regulations called laws. These laws existed in nature and humanity and were given to us as the natural and moral codes to relate with Him as the creator. These contain His perfect instructions to guide you to what to do and what not to do.

The root of spiritual and moral evil is traceable to human disobedience of the laws of God. Forsaking these laws leads to a breakdown at some point. Breaking the law of God switches off your heaven. When your heavens are switched off, you can be afflicted and molested by the devil. He also gains access into your heart to manipulate you. When your heavens are switched off, your spiritual communication line is cut off because God has no intimate relationship with law breakers. You need to switch on your heavens by repenting, confessing, and forsaking your sins. Ask God for forgiveness and mercy.

> ***"Repent, then, and turn to God, so that your sins may be wiped out, that times of refreshing may come from the Lord, and that he may send the Christ, who has been appointed for you-even Jesus"***
>
> ***-Acts 3:19***

God is the ultimate law giver; He wants you to obey His Word. Daniel knew that disobeying the voice of God was like disobeying the laws put in place to protect human life and properties. The best way to address the problem of national and universal moral evil is to allow the Word of God to shape human life and spiritual, political, social and scientific ideologies.

3. Prayer of Purification (Daniel 9:15-17)

Daniel prayed for forgiveness, mercy and favour of God for the restoration of Israel. He understood the principle, practice and power of prayer. He knew that humans have right to exercise yet human rights that isolate God's principles of moral standard would lead to a reprobate mind. Daniel used the power of prayer to restore lives from death, to reveal and interpret dreams, to rise to national leadership in Babylon, to conquer kingdoms after kingdoms, to defeat deadly lions in the den, and to retrieve future revelation from God's database. You too can pray your way out of moral, spiritual, financial career, marital, psychological, spiritual or mental captivity. You can pray like Daniel did.

4. Prayer of Restoration (Daniel 9:18-19)

Daniel prayed for the restoration of God's presence in Israel, His people's heart and the temple and its worship. Daniel knew that God had the ultimate control over the human heart, human life and the society. He holds the future in His hand and He knows what He is going to do next. Godly prayers are guided by these prayer patterns. You will experience God's divine presence if you learn to praise God, pray for purification and in filling of the Holy Spirit and if you spend more time praying for the restoration of sinners from their sinful ways. Prosperity, selfishness, greed, sin and hollow philosophy have switched off the heavens in many people's lives. The Church needs to pray for the restoration of God's presence in their places of worship.

POINTS ON PRAYER

- The key that unlocks your heavens in prayer no matter your situation is realising that God's covenant of love is with you.
- Acknowledging your wrongdoing when you are praying is vital to attracting God's forgiveness and favour.
- Whatever your problems, your faith in the miraculous power of God is sufficient to help you out.

Chapter 10

Jesus Christ and the Power of Prayer

THE LIFE, MINISTRY and miracles of Jesus Christ centred on His Word and prayer life. He knew that the best and only way to maintain constant conversation and communion with His Father was by prayer. He maintained the habit of personal and constant prayer fellowship with His heavenly Father.

"During the days of Jesus' life on earth, He offered up prayers and petitions with fervent cries and tears to the one who could save him from death, and he was heard because of his reverent submission. Son though he was, he learned obedience from what he suffered and, once made perfect, he became the source of eternal salvation for all who obey him and was designated by God to be high priest in the order of Melchizedek"

-Hebrews 5:7-10

Let us now consider Jesus' views and teachings on prayer.

"And when you pray, do not be like the hypocrites, for they love to pray standing in the synagogues and on the street corners to be seen by others. Truly I tell you, they have received their reward in full. But when you pray, go into your room, close the door and pray to your Father, who is unseen. Then your Father, who sees what is done in secret, will reward you. And when you pray, do not keep on babbling like pagans, for they think they will be heard because of their many words. Do not be like them, for your Father knows what you need before you ask him. This, then, is how you should pray: Our

> ***Father in heaven, hallowed be your name, your kingdom come, your will be done, on earth as it is in heaven. Give us today our daily bread. And forgive us our debts, as we also have forgiven our debtors. And lead us not into temptation, but deliver us from the evil one. For if you forgive other people when they sin against you, your heavenly Father will also forgive you. But if you do not forgive others their sins, your Father will not forgive your sins"***
>
> ***-Matthew 6:5-15***

Jesus' prayer lessons to His disciples and to the Church cover nine specific areas that need to be critically examined. If you think of the greatest prayer warrior that ever existed, Jesus Christ our Lord is the one. If you carefully study Jesus' life here on Earth, His relationship with His Father and His disciples, you will observe that Jesus spent most of His time in prayer. Mark recorded that *'Very early in the morning, while it was still dark, Jesus got up, left the house and went off to a solitary place, where he prayed.'*(Mark 1:35). While He was praying, His disciples were looking for Him because they wanted Him to preach and perform more miracles. But Jesus knew that the place to preach, the message to preach and the power to heal came from His Father. He went into solitary places seeking His Father's will for the next assignment.

After the miraculous multiplication of bread and fishes to feed about 5,000 people, besides women and children, Jesus dismissed the crowd, sent His disciples to the other side of the sea, and went to the mountainside to pray on His own (Matthew 14:23-24). After the prayer, Jesus went out to His disciples walking on the lake. He later commanded Peter to walk on the water towards Him. Jesus' prayer points were veiled here but it could be argued that He went into prayer to discuss issues with His Father. Jesus received His Father's approval to suspend the law of floatation. If the world was created by His powerful Word, He had the authority to suspend the law of nature.

Jesus was the Word through which Moses parted the Red Sea, and the Word through which Joshua parted the Jordan River. His disciples eventually discovered that prayer is more than ritual, recitation of prayers and sacrifices of the Jews. They realised prayer is a conversation with God who dwells in Heaven but control the affairs of the Earth. One day Jesus was praying in a certain place. When He finished praying, one of His disciples said to Him, 'Lord', teach us to pray, just as John taught his disciples' (Luke 11:1). His disciples wanted to know more about prayer and the secret of His miraculous power. Jesus' prayer involves nine distinct aspects.

Our Father in Heaven

Jesus teaches that the knowledge and revelation of your heavenly Father is crucial to your prayer life. The depth of your knowledge of Him, His will and desire, His love and compassion, His power and provisions, and His plan and purposes for your life are important factors that deepens your prayer life. You need to know God as the creator and sustainer of the universe. You need to see Him as the one who is in charge of powers and authority in the heavenly places and the one who is above all powers and principalities.

Paul the Apostle revealed that " *In Him we live and move and have our being*"(Acts 17:28).Without God, there is no life, movement or existence.You derive your sustenance from Him each day. He is the Alpha and the Omega, the beginning and the end of life itself. 'Our Father in heaven' is an affirmative statement that confesses that He is there for you, and His plan and purposes are intact. The statement reveals the care and love of God for you every day. When David stood before Goliath, he knew that he was not standing there alone. He knew that God the Father of Israel was standing there with him. He whispered the words of victory into his mind. David did not have time to waste in prayer. He confessed his Father's whisper in his mind; he declared it by his mouth. Goliath was defeated and Israel was delivered from harassment. (1 Samuel 17:45-47)

'Our Father in heaven' revealed God as all powerful and one who has control over all human affairs. He is the one who changes things at His will. The knowledge of God's identity could blow off your carnal mind in prayer, suppress your selfishness and inspire your zeal for praise and worship. It is a statement of intimacy, communion and connection. It is a statement that confirms the reality of God as being the one who speaks out the creation, the one who speaks to us through his Son, the one who cares for us each day and the one who satisfies the needs of the world.

What a wonderful day you will have when you wake up in the morning and remember that there is a loving Father who cares for you. This phrase affirms that humans are not descendants of apes or baboons but the grand product of God's creative Word. Our 'Father in heaven' is a statement that sparks a direct confident approach to God and His merciful outreach to humanity.

Hallowed Be Your Name

The word 'hallowed' means 'reverence', 'holy' or 'sanctified'. The names of God are linked to His revelation in Word and works of miracles to His people. He said to Moses, 'I AM WHO I AM' (Exodus 3:14). The phrase 'I AM' stands for God who does not change in nature, character, and promises. He said to Moses that, "I AM', who spoke to Abraham and I am ready to fulfil that promise through you now. This is my appointed time to deliver Israel from Egypt and to take them to the land I promised to Abraham and his descendants."

God's name plays an important role in the Scripture. He puts His name in places to bear His name, protects and delivers by His name, and acts for the sake of His name. Everything a believer will be depends on His name. Believers are identified with God by their faith in the name of Jesus. You are commanded to pray and worship in that name as God only identifies His power and presence with the name of Jesus. God has given Jesus a name that is above every other name and at the mention of this name, every knee must bow and every tongue must confess the name before the Almighty (Philippians 2:9-11).

To hallow this name in prayer means to trust and confess this name with honour and in respect to what He has revealed, what He has done and what He would do through this mighty name. Jesus uses the title 'I AM' to reveal to us that He was the one who spoke to Moses in the wilderness; He is the Word that is from the beginning; He is the Word that is the same yesterday and today and forever more (Hebrew 13:8). His name stands for the ownership of your life and existence, and His dominion over the affairs in Heaven and on Earth.

The name of Jesus Christ is identified as the 'Great Light 'Wonderful', 'Counsellor', 'Mighty God', 'Everlasting Father' an 'Prince of Peace' (Isaiah 9:2, 6). God is light and in Him there is n darkness. Jesus declared, He is the light of the world (John 8:12). Go packaged Jesus Christ with all the above qualities and those who ha Jesus Christ in their lives can experience His powerful presence i His written and revealed Word. You therefore need to hallow H name because He has lightened your heart when you were in darkne counselled you when you were confused; He used His mighty pow to deliver you from your foes; He granted you eternal life and ga you peace in unfathomable measure. To hallow the name of God is confess and actualize these spiritual benefits in your life at all tim. The name of the Lord is a strong tower, and the righteous run to and they are safe (Proverb 18:10). If God is holy, perfect and righteo, His name must therefore be set apart, honoured and reverenced. H name must be worshipped in prayer.

All the attributes of God and His mighty deeds in our lives must remembered and honoured. His name is to be adored and exalt above every other name. He has chosen to put His name in the tem built by King Solomon (2 Chronicles 7:11-12) as a response to s prayers for Israel. The name of the Lord implies His glorious prese and act of love towards His people. Jesus' name gives you the righ be in God's presence without fear. Jesus told His disciples: *"Whate you ask in my name I will do so that the Son may bring glory to t Father"*(John 14:13). Thus in prayer, you declare the praise and th worship of God as reflected in His name and attributes. When Jes said 'hallowed be your name', He means God is at work in your life every time and He will continue to work out His plan and purposes in your life with His mighty power and presence. Praising and worshiping God put you in the right frame of mind to approach God in prayer.

Your Kingdom Come

There is no kingdom without a king and there is no king without a kingdom. Matthew the evangelist mentioned the Kingdom of God or the kingdom of Heaven several times in his record of Jesus life and ministry. In Matthew 2:2, he referred to the king of the Jews whose star was seen by the wise men. At Jesus' crucifixion, there was an inscription 'King of the Jews' on His cross. John the Baptist introduced his preaching ministry by referring to the Kingdom that is near (Matthew 3:2). Jesus Christ after his Baptism declared that His ministry was about the Kingdom of God that is near (Matthew 4:17). Jesus used at least 30 different parables to teach about the Kingdom of God. In His prayer lesson to His disciples, the word 'Heaven' and 'Kingdom' of God reflected. His disciples also asked some striking questions about the Kingdom of God, 'who is the greatest in the Kingdom of Heaven?' (Matthew 18:1).

For Matthew to refer to the Kingdom in this way, then the issue of the Kingdom of Heaven must be vital to Jesus, His dominion in Heaven and His ministry on Earth. It is important to study the Kingdom of Heaven and understand what it is all about. If Jesus is the King as stated by the wise men, then He must have a kingdom. If He declared that the Kingdom of God is near and that people should repent to belong to this Kingdom, then it is essential to understand the mission, its fulfilment, its expansion and why Jesus prayed for its coming.

DEFINITION OF TERMS

After the record of Jesus' birth, Matthew referred to Jesus as the born

King of the Jews (Matthew 2:2). When Pilate the governor asked Jesus, 'Are you the king of the Jews?", He answered "Yes you are right." Therefore the word 'king' to Jesus, Herod, the Jews, the Roman Empire, the Pharisees and the Roman governor is crucial, significant and full of different meanings. The preaching of John, Jesus and the disciples of Jesus focused on 'the kingdom that was near.' What are the meanings of these words used by Jesus and Matthew?

Literarily, a king is a male sovereign over a nation or territory; a higher rank over any other ruler except an emperor. The community may concentrate all spiritual and political power in his sovereignty. In the past, some kings were regarded as semi-god or semi-divine representative of God on Earth. Others were regarded as gods, or supernatural being. Spiritually, God is considered as the King above all kings of the earth (Psalm 2:2). Heaven is the dwelling place of God. He is everywhere but He makes Himself present in certain places on the Earth to bless. Earth is a place in the universe and Heaven is considered as linked with the Earth in the spiritual realm. Heaven is an unknown but real location where God dwells.

Wayne Grudem, Professor of Biblical and Systematic Theology defined heaven as "A place, not just a state of mind. It is an undiscovered world testified by the Scripture. It is a real place." The Kingdom of Heaven or the kingdom of God is of God, a place where God reigns in His spiritual realm. If God is Spirit (John 4:23), then His kingdom, His reign, His authority, His dominion and His government is a spiritual reality. Only those who have the Spirit of God can understand the things of the Spirit. The Kingdom of God is also considered as the eventual fulfilment of God's will on Earth. The idea of God as King was common to Judaism and the Jewish idea of the kingdom of God most likely shaped the New Testament usage.

Louis Berkhof, Professor of Systematic Theology defined the Kingdom of God "as the rule of God established and acknowledged in the hearts of sinners by the regenerating influence of the Holy Spirit, ensuring them of the blessings of salvation, a rule that is realised in principle on Earth, but will not reach its culmination until the return of Jesus Christ." The kingdom is spiritual and invisible in nature. Matthew referred to two kings in Chapter 2 of his gospel. But can two kings reign in one kingdom? During the time of Jesus, Herod the Great was the king over Israel. He was a political king but not a Jew. He was chosen by the Roman Empire and was in charge of Judea, Galilee, and Samaria. As a powerful king, he was filled with threat to his authority when he heard that the King of the Jews was born and he tried his wicked plan to get rid of the born King of the Jews.

While Herod was a political king, Jesus was a prophetic king that reigned on the throne of David. The prophets saw this divine plan of God and declared it to Israel. Prophet Jeremiah referred to this king as David's righteous branch, the wise, righteous and just king and 'The Lord our Righteousness' (Jeremiah 23:5-6). Isaiah saw this king as a child that is born and His name is called Wonderful counsellor, Mighty God, Everlasting Father, Prince of Peace. He will reign on David's throne and over His kingdom (Isaiah 9:6-7). Jesus' title as king could therefore never mean a political title or an office but a divine fulfilment of God's divine plan for David, Israel and the entire world.

Therefore when Jesus announced the Kingdom of heaven in His preaching and asked for its coming in His prayer, He was saying that the knowledge, presence, will and relationship with God that was lost by Adam and Eve in the Garden of Eden was about to be restored on Earth. The Word that came to Adam and Eve in Eden at the cool of the day has arrived again on Earth to restore all things. 'Your Kingdom come' therefore implies the invitation of God's reign into your life and affairs, the invitation of God's presence, authority and dominion into your life, the invitation of God's Spirit and full blessings of salvation and peace into your life and also the invitation of God's absolute influence into your life.

The kingdom that Jesus announced was an immediate one that extends into the future. It was a kingdom that is real in His person and ministry. His ministry and His miracles implied that the great future expected by the Jews had started. Jesus was sent by God to inaugurate the Kingdom of God on Earth. Whenever Jesus spoke of the Kingdom of God or Kingdom of Heaven, He was referring to where He came from. Jesus' teachings are not from man but from the one He brings from Heaven where He came from. His message is the original copy of what was given to Moses on Mount Sinai as the Ten Commandments. This is why Jesus said that He did not come to abolish the Law but to fulfil it. 'Your kingdom come' in Jesus' prayer lessons points to the presence of God taking absolute control of your life and prayer activities. You need God as you don't know what to pray for and don't have the power to bring results to your prayer requests. Jesus was saying that the presence of God is all you need to offer the right prayers and to obtain the right answers at all times.

Jesus' miracles were not magic. The sight, healings, and deliverances that He gave to the sick were not medically designed; they were from the origin of life and existence. As Jesus spoke, the miracles happened. According to Marshall, 'the kingdom of heaven breaks into the domain of evil to restore God's will on Earth and the power of Satan is broken. Jesus sees him fall like lightning from heaven' (Marshall I. H 1996, New Bible Dictionary page 648). All authority in Heaven and on Earth has been given to the King of kings and Jesus has given power to the Church to cast out devil and to heal the sick (Mark 16:16-18). The Church can therefore heal the world from sin, sickness and evil through the Word of God and prayer. You too, can tap into the realm of God's Kingdom by faith and prayer to receive power to destroy all the works of the devil and actualise the plans and purposes of God for your life, family, community and the nations.

If God created the universe, and man in His image, and gives the universe to man as his domain, God wants to relate with man in managing the universe according to His divine plan and purpose through His Spirit. Jesus referred to a kingdom that exists from the beginning of the world. The kingdom is now near through His person and ministry and in us through His Spirit.

Jesus emphasised the presence and power of God in the Kingdom He came to establish, spiritually, ethically and socially. Jesus taught about the life that conforms to the nature of God in the Kingdom. Jesus taught about the ability to make choices by the power of the Holy Spirit to fulfil the purpose of God in creation. The Kingdom is present and continues into the future with God's power in you, the Church and the world. The reign of God in the hearts of believers and unbelievers is more important than social reformation. Social or prosperity gospel without spiritual transformation equals political manipulation and building of personal kingdom. The Kingdom that Jesus preached and prayed is more important than a political kingdom. It is a Kingdom where God is the King; the Kingdom that brings peace as predicted by Prophet Isaiah and declared by Jesus.

Why did Jesus come to establish the Kingdom of God and refer to it in His prayers? For the sake of clarity and the link between Jesus' ministry and the Old Testament, it is important to examine the purpose and the duty of Israel as a nation to God and to the world. God declared His assignment to Israel through Moses in (Exodus 19: 5-6). *'Now if you obey me fully and keep my covenant, then out of all nations you will be my treasured possession. Although the whole earth is mine, you will be for me a kingdom of priests and a holy nation.'*God chose Israel to teach the nations His will and ways but they failed in this divine task.

Asaph, the psalmist revealed that the responsibility of Israel is to teach the next generation about the ways and deeds of God. But Israel failed to do so, maybe because they neglected their duty of prayer and teaching of the Word. Asaph declared:

> ***"I will open my mouth in parables, I will utter hidden things, things from of old, what we have heard and known, what our fathers have told us. We will not hide them from their children, we will tell the next generation the praiseworthy deeds of the Lord, his power, and the wonders he has done. He decreed statutes for Jacob and established law in Israel, which he commanded our forefathers to teach the children, so the next generation would know them, even the children yet unborn***

and they in turn would tell their children then they would put their trust in God and would not forget his deeds but would keep his commands"

-Psalm 78:2-7

The Psalmist confirmed that Israel neglected their responsibility because they had turned the house of prayer into a market and a den of robbers (John 2:13-16; Matthew 21:13). God decided to raise His own Son to fill the gap. Israel forsook the Word of God, the way of God, the will of God and prayer to God. Therefore God gave them over to the gentile nations. James Luther said that "God's way and will are essential elements of reality and Israel was ordained for this very purpose to teach other nations." The way God led Israel from Egypt and how He raised Prophets among them suggests that God designed a theocratic Kingdom in order to lead and guide them in His divine purpose.

The reign of God is crucial to Israel nation, but they broke this covenant when they reached the Promise Land. The purposes of God were abandoned by the Israelites in the past, and the same is true in the world today. Many people now consider God and His Words irrelevant to the needs of this generation. It is like saying that life is not relevant to living whereas there is no living without life. Living without the fullness of God's life in us is to be lifeless.

At the time of Jesus, people have teachers of the law but misinterpreted and misunderstood it. They questioned Jesus about the law but He told them that He did not come to abolish the law but to fulfil it. Jesus' teaching started from the introduction of the kingdom of God that is near (Matthew 4:17), the condition of belonging to it and its lifestyle. Jesus used parable to bring His message to the understanding of His hearers but they could not interpret the Word of God. The apostles who will bring the message of the Kingdom to other nations sought the true meaning and understanding of Jesus' mission. Jesus equipped and trained His disciples for this purpose; to preach and pray for the coming of the Kingdom of God. Jesus' mission is to recruit the priests to teach the nations the way and the will of God, not to build a political kingdom as supposed by some people. Jesus came to build the Church - the community of God's people and God's kingdom.

Jesus gave His Kingdom's authority to His first Church and today's Church to proclaim the Kingdom's message to the entire world, starting from Jerusalem. Why Jerusalem? God made Jerusalem the reference point where He intended to raise priests to teach the nation. Jesus said salvation is from the Jews, extended to the gentiles. Now the gentiles that turned to Jesus share the same blessings promised to Abraham's descendants. Therefore, because the authority of the Kingdom has been delegated to the first disciples, they preached the gospel, healed the sick and performed miracles like Jesus. That same authority is still available in the Church today.

Power and authority have been given to Christians to pray the will of God into existence. This authority supersedes political or scientific authority because Jesus' Word is alive and active. Jesus is the Word that created all things; the Word that became flesh, and the Word that lives forever. There is no opposition to this powerful Word; no force can stop it from coming to pass. Jesus did not need any medical intervention to heal the sick because the authority that Jesus used to create is the same authority He used to heal and perform miracles. The purpose of God through the Church is therefore crucial to every kingdom and nation of the world.

The kingdom of God is not about where you live, what you eat, or what you drink, but a matter of righteousness and elimination of evil from the human heart and society. Jesus' Kingdom is within us. (Luke17:21). God intends to reign among us and within us as He did with the Israelites in the wilderness. He wants to reign among nations and kingdoms of the world today. The Church is the extension of the kingdom of God on Earth and its role is to embark on declaring the reign of God, teaching the way of the Almighty and showing the way of peace to the nations. The world and man cannot live God's purpose without the reign of God. The kingdom of God is here right now and we can feel it through the power of the Holy Spirit in the Church. The gospel of the Kingdom and its application is therefore the answer to the challenges of the 21st Century.

Jesus linked prayer to the Kingdom of God to teach His disciples that prayer is not the business of carnal people. It is a spiritual assignment with the Almighty God. John the Baptist testified about Jesus saying that 'the one who comes from above is above all. He testified to what he has seen and heard, but no one accepted his testimony' (John 3:31-32). Prayer has to do with feeling, hearing, knowing and seeing, but you cannot hear, know or see if you are not filled with the presence of God when you pray. Prayer is not an "Earth to Heaven" conversation; it is a "heart to heart" conversation with God through His Spirit and His Word in your heart. Prayer is not about shouting; it is about sharing views in the realm of the spirit.

During prayer at home one day, my children asked me: "Daddy, you always say God speaks to you; how do you hear God speak when you don't see Him?" Believers face similar problems when it comes to prayer. Initially I found it difficult to explain this experience to my children because of their age and Christian experience. I then asked them: "If I am in the garden and called you, can you hear me? They cheerily said yes". Can you see me? They said no because there is a wall and door barrier. I asked: "If you open the door and come to the garden will you be able to see and hear me?" They said yes. I said this is the same with God. He is invisible but He speaks to us through our mind when we are filled with His Spirit, and when we open the door of our hearts to Him in prayer.

Jesus linked prayer with the Kingdom of God because it is an act of worship. He observed that the Jews were prayerful but their hearts were far from God (Luke 18:9-14). There was dialogue and disagreement about the worship of God between the Jews and the Samaritans. Jesus spoke to the woman of Samaria who He met at Jacob's well and declared: "*You Samaritans worship what you do not know; we worship what we do know, for salvation is from the Jews. Yet a time is coming and has now come when the true worshippers will worship the Father in Spirit and truth, for they are the kind of worshippers the Father seeks. God is Spirit, and his worshippers must worship in Spirit and truth"* (John 4:22-24).

Prayer without adequate knowledge and purposes of God and His kingdom is like an orphan who has no parent to speak to in times of need. The knowledge of God's power, presence, provisions and ultimate plan for the present and the future is very vital to the worship of God and experience of God in prayer. God is not an idol who cannot speak; He was the one who spoke out the world and its fullness. The worship of God without the Word and full revelation of God in Christ Jesus is a mere fantasy. Like the Samaritans, many believers' worship in prayer lacks the revelation of God. Some believers think they can force God into their own personal agenda. You are wasting your time if you think you can do that.

Your prayer cannot change the mind of God. Your prayer can only change your mind to God's mind to know the purposes and plans of God for your life. Daniel the Prophet declared *'those who knew their God will do great exploits* (Daniel 11:33) . Worshipping God during prayer in spirit and truth is allowing God to take the lead and making way for His will to prevail. Aggressive prayer without adequate revelation of God's being, His power and presence would only amount to an emotional exercise. Aggressive prayer with adequate knowledge of God is what produces great result. Jesus linked prayer to the kingdom of God because He is seeking for those who will pray with sincere and humble spirit, and those who will be still in God's presence and know that He is God.

Jesus differentiates between honest and holy prayer from hypocritical prayers. The hypocrites see prayer as criteria for religious identity in order to impress people. Jesus said they have received their reward in full (Matthew 6:5). Jesus sees prayer as an expression of relationship between you and your heavenly Father. God tells you what have been done in secret that need to be manifested (Matthew 6:5-6). The will of God and the will of man must agree in prayer in order to manifest uncommon results.

Your will be done on Earth as it is in Heaven

Prayer involvcs the will of two or more people. Will is defined as the mental power by which you control your thought, actions and decisions. Personal prayer involves the will of God and the will of the one who is praying. Congregational prayer involves the will of God and the will of the congregation in prayer. Jesus' prayer session at Gethsemane revealed the will of Jesus and the will of God in prayer. Jesus was in Gethsemane to confirm the will of God for the price He needed to pay for the sin of the world (Matthew 26:39-42).

At Lazarus' tomb, Jesus raised his eyes unto Heaven and said:

> ***"Father, I thank you that you have heard me. I knew that you always hear me, but I said this for the benefit of the people standing here, that they may believe that you sent me. When he had said this, Jesus called in a loud voice, 'Lazarus, come out!' The dead man came out, his hands and feet wrapped with strips of linen, and a cloth around his face. Jesus said to them, take off the grave clothes and let him go."***
>
> ***-John 11:41-44***

That was a congregational prayer with Jesus and the people at Lazarus tomb. Jesus may have joined hands with Mary and Martha and His disciples and prayed like this: "God, raise Lazarus from the dead" or "God, accept Lazarus soul into Heaven" or "God, please reveal to us what killed Lazarus, or "God rebuke Satan over the family of Lazarus". We don't know exactly what happened but the secret of the power of prayer in that scenario was that Jesus has met God to discuss Lazarus' death and God told Him, "Go and wake him up." That was God's will for Lazarus. The will of God and Jesus came to pass in the life of Lazarus and his family. Lazarus came back to life after he died and was buried for four days. The will of God in prayer is very crucial to God's response to our prayers. Therefore, the will of God on Earth is more important than our own will in prayer.

The statement 'your will be done on earth as it is in heaven' implies that the will of God for our lives and on earth has been pre-determined by God before we were created. God told Jeremiah the prophet "*Before I formed you in the womb I knew you, before you were born I set you apart; I appointed you as a prophet to the nations*" (Jeremiah 1:5). King David proclaimed that "*My frame was not hidden from you when I was made in the secret place. When I was woven together in the depths of the earth, your eyes saw my unformed body. All days ordained for me were written in your book before one of them came to be*"(Psalm 139:15-16).

You need to ask for God's will in every situation before you start to release your will in prayer. No matter how long you pray, God has the final say in all matters of life. You pray, but He gives answer. No wonder Paul the Apostle advised us: "*Do not be anxious about anything, but in everything, by prayer and petition, with thanksgiving, present your requests to God. And the peace of God, which transcends all understanding, will guard your hearts and your minds in Christ Jesus*"(Philippians 4:6-8).

The will of God is manifested in the words and works of Jesus Christ. His prayer life centred on these two principles: The Word of God, the will of God and the work of God are crucial to your prayer life and you need the Spirit of God to discern them. Jesus came from Heaven to do His Father's will on Earth, and He came to speak on His Father's behalf. When He prayed, He sought for the heavenly will to be carried out on Earth. Therefore, linking prayer to God's will means the will of God must be at the heart of your prayer life. You are to seek the will of God first in His Word in prayer and then confess and claim it by faith.

Give Us This Day our Daily Bread

> ***"He waters the mountains from His upper chambers; the earth is satisfied by the fruit of His work. He makes the grass grow for the cattle, and plants for man to cultivate, bringing forth food from the earth"***
>
> ***-Psalm 104:13-14***

All we do as humans is to advance in technology through wisdom and knowledge, to expand and increase what God has given us in naturc. Our responsibility as human being is to obey the law of seed and harvest. Whatever method you want to adopt, whether manual or mechanised farming, you need to plant the seed, care for it, supply the necessary nutrients and nurture it. You then pray to God for rain and good weather to make the plant grow. 'Give us this day our daily bread' simply implies that everything we need to 'grow' comes from God. We need to thank Him for all His free supplies and ask Him to give us more. No wonder the Psalmist says:

> ***"He sends the springs into the valleys they flow among the hills. They give drink to every beast of the field; the wild donkeys quench their thirst. By them the birds of the heavens have their home; they sing among the branches. He waters the hills from His upper chambers; the earth is satisfied with the fruit of your works. He causes the grass to grow for the cattle, And vegetation for the service of man, That he may bring forth food from the earth, And wine that makes glad the heart of man, Oil to make his face shine, And bread which strengthens man's heart. The trees of the Lord are full of sap, the cedars of Lebanon which He planted, where the birds make their nests; the stork has her home in the fir trees. The high hills are for the wild goats; the cliffs are a refuge for the rock badgers. He appointed the moon for seasons; the sun knows it's going down. You make darkness, and it is night, in which all the beasts of the forest creep about. The young lions roar after their prey, and seek their food from God. When the sun rises, they gather together and lie down in their dens. Man goes out to his work and to his labour until the evening. O Lord, how manifold is your works! In wisdom you have made them all. The earth is full of your possessions"***
>
> ***-Psalm 104:10-24***

The Psalmist revealed God's richness in His wisdom, goodness, love, and care for His creation. Every living thing was created by God to depend on creator for living. He gave us wisdom, talents and abilities to care for each other and the nature around us. Everything we see around us speaks of the greatness and goodness of God daily. He is the maker of all things; we make bread, wine, ointments, fruit juices, cars, ships, aeroplanes, clothing, and shoes from what He has already made.

Greediness and selfishness are the causes of poverty in some parts of the world. The miracle of the multiplied bread and fishes by Jesus Christ to feed thousands of people in the wilderness implies that God knows about everything we lack and need, and has solutions to these needs at every moment of our lives. He has given us everything we need to live here on earth. The boy who had five small loaves of barley and two small fishes gave it up to Jesus to provide for the needs of thousands of hungry souls (John 6:5-14).

What a contrast to what we witness in the Church and in the world today. Ministers of God are lining their pockets at the expense of their poor members, and politicians are splashing thousands of pounds on holidays at the expense of struggling working families. The inequalities that exist in society today are not the plan of God but the result of sinful human greed. While we pray for our daily bread, we need to channel God's distribution when such blessings come. God's supply each day is more than enough to feed the world if selfish ambition, greed and lust for wealth are removed from human mindset.

Forgive us our sins, as we forgive those who sin against us

TheScripture refers to two main types of sins: the sin against God and the sin against one another. One common sin in the world today is to believe and teach that there is no God, and that God is not the creator of all things. Theologians called this teaching 'ATHEISM' and the teaching is spreading rapidly in the West. This belief coupled with the theory of evolution have placed human mind in the realm of aggressive secularism, rebellion and depravity.

The depraved mind relies only on human knowledge and wisdom as the only source of ideas and experience; hence knowledge and wisdom are being recycled from one generation to another. Humanity is taking the place of God in life affairs; the search for knowledge is discarding the revelation of God's knowledge in creation and nature. Feeble minds conclude that "if God cannot be proved in the scientific laboratory, then He doesn't exist." Let me humbly argue that God is not a matter that can be studied by experiment. He is Spirit that is real and exists (John 4:24). God can only be known through faith in His revealed Word (John 1:1).

The God of the Bible cannot be known in the laboratory and the god of the laboratory cannot be compared with the God of the Bible. The god of the laboratory is an imagined god; the God of the Bible is the creator of knowledge and the scientists. The god of the laboratory is an invented god of this age, who according to Paul the apostle *"Has blinded the minds of unbelievers, so that they cannot see the light of the gospel of the glory of Christ who is the image of God"* (2 Corinthian 4:4). Therefore whenever you replaced God with any invented god in form of images, objects, knowledge, philosophy or belief, you have sinned against Almighty.

Moses had this to say to the children of Israel:

> ***"The upright one grew fat and kicked; filled with food, he became heavy and sleek. He abandoned the God who made him and rejected the Rock his Saviour. They made him jealous with their foreign gods and angered him with their detestable idols. They sacrificed to demons, which are not God."***
>
> ***-Deuteronomy 32:15-17***

Secularism and our post-modern world multi-religious society have placed the Almighty God, idols and demons on the same platform. We are living in a world where whatever you worship or believe is right or do seem to be right as humans. Individuals are increasingly putting facts above the absolute truth of God's Word. The moral absolute of God is being eroded by post-modern philosophers and thinkers. This sin of apostasy needs to be confessed and we must ask God for forgiveness. The world is heading to a moral, spiritual and social disaster as the creation is being detached from the creator. The world will not find peace without the prince of peace!

The sins against others result from breaking the golden rule of God as stated in the Bible. These sins are the result of actions contrary to what is good, right and lovely to others around us. The reprobate mind lusts for doing what is evil, wicked, hateful, hurtful and disastrous to our fellow human. Paul the apostle describes the attitude of sinners against each other this way:

> ***"There is no one righteous, not even one; there is no one who understands, no one seeks God. All have turned away; they have together become worthless; there is no one who does good, not even one. Their throats are open graves; their tongues practice deceit. The poison of vipers is on their lips. Their mouths are full of cursing and bitterness. Their feet are swift to shed blood; ruin and misery mark their ways, and the way of peace they do not know. There is no fear of God before their eyes."***
>
> ***-Romans 3:10-18***

The wrong use of your tongue, words, feet, hands and body to harm yourself and others is not acceptable to God or society. Good and bad, right and wrong, evil and wickedness is inherent in human heart. James the apostle confirms that wrong desires gives birth to death. Sinful habits are unacceptable before God and they need to be confessed for your prayer to be powerful and effective.

Jesus teaches that if you don't forgive others their sins, God will not forgive you your own sins (Matthew 6:14-15). Forgiving others reminds you of God's continuous forgiveness and love towards you. It deepens your relationship with God and others, and clears your mind from spiritual stains that can block the whisper of the Holy Spirit.

Forgiveness draws God's presence in prayer, releases His power and will into your consciousness. It enhances the time of refreshment with God. It puts your prayer life into God's perspective through His Word, helps you to pray for others, gives you love for those who do you wrong and enables you to sympathise with the weak and the frail. Forgiving others heal your heart from wicked thoughts and evil scheme.

Lead us not into temptation, but deliver us from the evil one

The words 'temptation' and 'evil' are vital in the above statement. Temptation simply means testing with evil intent. You must assess your mind capacity in order to discover and the devil using your weaknesses to trap you to do his will. The tempter draws you into wrong desires and impulses. The devil uses the power of manipulation to tempt you to desert God's will and agenda. Satan was allowed by God to tempt Job and Jesus in different circumstances. Job was tempted, and God allowed Satan to destroy his possessions. Jesus was tempted into turning stone to bread and gain the entire world's possession if He submitted to Satan's authority. Both temptations were aimed at making Job and Jesus desert God's will. Both of them were led into temptation in order to prove God's faithfulness to His Word and purposes.

Satan's target during temptation is to make you fall from God's grace, will and divine plan during difficult situations. Job was tempted through the wealth he had and Jesus was tempted after he was led into the wilderness by the Holy Spirit to fast for 40 days and 40 nights. Both Job and Jesus were pillars of faith, piety and holiness. But Satan wanted them to do wrong through natural desires. In the case of Job, his wife asked him to curse God and die. Satan wanted Jesus to turn stone to bread, and to jump from the pinnacle of the temple, and submit to his authority. But this authority has been given to Jesus Christ from creation.

Jesus told Satan, "you don't need to test me whether I am the son of God; I know who I am. I am the Word that created all things from the beginning, and that includes you Satan. You don't need to tell me to turn stone to bread; I can make bread from nothing. The Word that makes bread does not require stone! I don't manipulate my Word to make bread. I am the bread of life!" Jesus told Satan, that the Word of God cannot put God to test as the Word of God cannot do what is contrary to God's will. Satan tried to reposition Jesus in the realm of spiritual authority as he did to Adam in the Garden of Eden, but his attempt failed because the Word that created Satan was greater and above Satan. Jesus told him " *Away from me, Satan! For it is written: Worship the Lord, and serve him only"* (Matthew 4:1-11).

When Jesus taught His disciples to pray: 'lead us not into temptation but deliver us from the evil one', He was telling them that the evil one is real in our world, and has an agenda to distract, disrupt, destroy and disconnect humanity from the plan and purposes of God. Today Satan has come up with his doctrines and teachings, equipping false teachers, using them to distort the truth, teaching people what is evil as normal behaviour for Christians and non - Christians to practise. False ideas of God's truth have led to the mis-interpretation and mis-applying of the Word of God but there is no other truth beside the one revealed in the scriptures.

We live with good and evil, right and wrong every time, and Satan uses evil desires and motives to tempt our minds. In the moment of trial, testing and temptation, the measure of truth that you have is what determines the level of your victory. Jesus declared: "*You will know the truth and the truth will set you free"* (John 8:32). It was not only prayer and fasting that Jesus used to defeat Satan; He applied the Word of truth, the two edged sword that cut into pieces the motives of Satan. If you saturate your heart with the Word of God, you will be able to resist evil desires and impulses as they come to your mind.

God may allow you to experience temptation but He will not let you fall into it. Whenever God leads you into temptation, He is there to teach you a lesson. He is also there to deliver you and help you overcome the temptation as He did for Job and Jesus. When Satan leads you into temptation through evil desire, he entices and drags you away from the Word and the will God. If you allow the evil desire to germinate, it grows into sin and sin leads to death. It is Satan that prompts you to do what is wrong to gratify your selfish desires. Jesus is therefore teaching you to ask God not to expose you to temptation from Satan. He had prayed for you that God should protect you from the evil one (John 17:15).

The Audacity of Prayer (Luke 11:5-11; 18:1-8)

Then Jesus said to them,

> ***"Suppose you have a friend, and you go to him at midnight and say, 'Friend, lend me three loaves of bread; a friend of mine on a journey has come to me, and I have no food to offer him.' And suppose the one inside answers, 'Don't bother me. The door is already locked, and my children and I are in bed. I can't get up and give you anything.' I tell you, even though he will not get up and give you the bread because of friendship, yet because of your shameless audacity he will surely get up and give you as much as you need. So I say to you: Ask and it will be given to you; seek and you will find; knock and the door will be opened to you. For everyone who asks receives; the one who seeks finds; and to the one who knocks, the door will be opened. "Which of you fathers, if your son asks for a fish, will give him a snake instead? Or if he asks for an egg, will give him a scorpion? If you then, though you are evil, know how to give good gifts to your children, how much more will your Father in heaven give the Holy Spirit to those who ask him?"***
>
> ***-Luke 11: 5-13***

After Jesus taught His disciples about prayer, He moved on to teach them the need to be persistent in prayer. He analysed His teaching using two stories of a friend and a father. From a true friend and family, there is true relationship, love, communication, help, support, and understanding. Jesus taught that there is a positive answer to persistent prayer born out of true friendship with God and His Word. He teaches you not to give up praying until you receive an answer. Pray until something happens. God is love and He is always willing to give you more than you asked for. Giving up hope to weakness and tiredness at the first trial in prayer limits the power and blessings of persistent prayer. King David said " *Evening, morning and noon I cry out in distress and he hears my voice. He ransomed me unharmed from the battle waged against me, even though many oppose me"* (Psalm 55:17-18).

David was saying that "three times a day I entered into meaningful conversation with God who is able to deliver me from all fears and distress." David knew how to ask, seek, and knock on God's heart with his requests. Paul the Apostle also advised us to pray continually (1 Thessalonians.5:17). Persistence in prayer requires continuous communion, communication and consciousness of God's presence through His Spirit in us. Thus we can pray all the time in the Spirit as Paul admonished Timothy:

> ***"I urge, then, first of all, that petitions, prayers, intercession and thanksgiving be made for all people—for kings and all those in authority, that we may live peaceful and quiet lives in all godliness and holiness. This is good, and pleases God our Saviour, who wants all people to be saved and to come to the knowledge of the truth. I want the men and women everywhere to lift up holy hands in prayer, without anger or disputing."***
>
> ***-1 Timothy 2:1-4, 8***

Persistence in prayer helps you feel God's presence within you, helps you to hear Him answering your prayers, guides you through His Word, assures you of His constant care and protection and ensures your peace in the midst of crises. The Lord also heals your pain, comfort you through His Spirit and lead you to His desired destination. Persistence in prayer means 'you want to hear what God is saying concerning your situation.' Like Jesus Christ, you can catch up with God plans and purposes for your life, ministry, family, community, nations and the world through persistent prayer.

Jesus prayed on the cross of Calvary; God allowed a fish to swallow up Jonah to pray in its belly (Jonah 2:1). David cried from the cave; Jacob wrestled with God all night and his name was changed from Jacob to Israel (Genesis 32:26-30). Daniel persisted in prayer for three weeks and overcame the prince of the Persia's kingdom that resisted answers to his prayer (Daniel 10:10-14); Paul and Silas never lost that sense of persistence in prayer even while in prison, and all of them were answered by our faithful God. Don't give up; arise and rekindle the spirit of prayer as your better days lie ahead!

POINTS ON PRAYER

- ☐ The knowledge and revelation of your heavenly Father is crucial to your prayer life.
- ☐ Praising and worshiping God put you in the right frame of mind to approach God in prayer.
- ☐ Power and authority have been given to Christians to pray the will of God into reality.

Chapter 11

The Early Church and the Power of Prayer

THE DISCIPLES OF Jesus Christ applied the teachings they received while the great Master teacher was with them. They did not pray occasionally; they saw prayer as a vital part of the mission Jesus committed into their hands. The apostles used the power of prayer to handle different challenges and difficult situations in their missionary work. As well as applying the power of prayer, they also prayed through the Holy Spirit. The apostles, who had experienced how Jesus prayed, used the power of prayer to perform miracles, signs and wonders. Having received instructions from their Master, they gave their attention to exercising the power of prayer. The apostles centred their attention on two major tasks: prayer and the spreading the Word. The apostles used the power of prayer at different occasions as outlined below.

> ***"And we will give our attention to prayer and the ministry of the Word."***
>
> ***Acts 6:4***

Church Leadership and the Power of Prayer

> ***"They all joined together constantly in prayer, along with the women and Mary the mother of Jesus, and with brothers."***
>
> ***-Acts 1:14***

There were 120 people in the first Church that Jesus left when He ascended to Heaven. The first thing His followers did after Jesus instructed them to go to Jerusalem to wait for the promise of the Father (the Holy Spirit) was to gather together in the upper room for constant prayer. While they waited for the Holy Spirit, they did not just gather together daily to celebrate the promise with eating and drinking, but also waited in constant prayer. They prayed and planned for the mission Jesus committed into their hands.

Through prayer, the apostles saw the events that surrounded the betrayal, arrest, trial, crucifixion, death, resurrection and ascension of Jesus Christ. They also saw the death of Judas Iscariot and the action of Judas as fulfilment of the scripture (Psalm 109:9). The apostles discovered that through prayer the position and ministry of Judas Iscariot needs to be filled. While James (Jesus' brother) and Mary (the mother of Jesus) were among the 120 disciples that gathered together in prayer in the upper room, they were not automatically elected to fill the position left by Judas. Instead, they joined constantly in prayer for the one chosen by God. Mary and James did not see Jesus' ministry as a family business but as God's business and that the will of God must prevail over all matters. The disciples followed in the footsteps of their Master and prayed just as Jesus prayed all night before choosing his first twelve disciples.

The disciples prayed before selecting people into leadership role. The one to replace Judas had to be someone who was a part of Jesus' ministry from the time of John the Baptist (Acts 1:21-22). Justus and Matthias from among the 120 disciples were selected using this criterion. The disciples then prayed to God to show them the one He had chosen among the two candidates. This was their prayer: *"Lord, you know everyone's heart. Show us which of these two you have chosen to take over this apostolic ministry, which Judas left to go to where he belongs"*(Acts 1:24-25).

The disciples had a desire for God's choice and were not motivated by political or financial gain. The heart of the leadership in the early Church was in apostolic mission and ministry. While they were waiting for the Holy Spirit, the disciples planned for the project Jesus had committed to their hands, and had no room for leadership conflict, competition, corruption and caucuses among them. They had sincere motive, clear focus, committed hearts, a unified vision, and concrete plan for the Great Commission.

Constant prayer ushered the disciples into the promise of the in-filling of the Holy Spirit at Pentecost. Jesus had instructed his followers to wait until they are clothed with power from on high (Luke 24:49). He told them they would receive power when the Holy Spirit comes on them and that they would be His witnesses in Jerusalem, Judea, Samaria, and to the ends of the Earth (Acts 1:8). The disciples received this promise through waiting and commitment to constant prayer.

The disciples were all in one place on the day of Pentecost when God released His Spirit on them (Acts 2:1). Pentecost, one of the three annual feasts held by the Jews, was thanksgiving for the harvested crops. Jews from many nations gathered together for this festival to celebrate. While other Jews were celebrating with wine and food rejoicing, the apostles were celebrating in constant prayer and worship to the God who gives harvest (Acts 2:13). Suddenly there was a divine manifestation of God's presence in the person of the Holy Spirit. The people were empowered to launch the mission of Jesus Christ and the preaching of repentance and forgiveness to all nations beginning from Jerusalem. The disciples prayed constantly for the power of the Holy Spirit to spread the gospel with boldness. The early Church was motivated into prayer by their burning passion and desire to advance God's kingdom. The Church today needs to learn a lesson from this passion and affect societies for God.

Persecution and the Power of Prayer

The early Church leaders were prayer giants. The practice of prayer, the preaching of the good news about Jesus Christ and regular fellowship were the things that expanded the early Church. Peter was not the one who prepared the first message at the first international crusade; it was the Holy Spirit that spoke through him. By the wisdom and inspiration of the Holy Spirit, Peter understood and experienced the empowerment of the Holy Spirit. Peter never recited written sermons; he did not link his sermons to Jewish tradition, but instead, he preached the revealed scripture.

Peter was able to summarize the life and ministry of Jesus Christ as predicted in the Jewish scripture, and concluded that the coming of the Holy Spirit was to testify to the truth that Jesus is the Saviour of the world. The Holy Spirit applied Peter's message to the hearts of his listeners; Peter did not use any logical means to win souls to God. Those 'converted' swelled in their numbers from 120 to about 3000 at the first open air crusade. They continued to fellowship together every day, devoting themselves to the apostles' teachings, breaking of bread, and to prayer (Acts 2:42).

The first converts were taught the importance of the apostles' doctrine, prayer, fellowship, study of the Bible and Holy Communion. I must ask: "What do we do to the new convert nowadays where mega churches and media gospel preachers did not even have direct contact with new converts?" How are we growing the faith of the post-modern believers? We can see the pattern of the first converts in the early Church; they were taught by the apostles, and were included in prayer meetings and fellowships. They needed to be in a group where they learnt the Word of God, prayed, and fellowshipped to mature in their faith.

The greatest danger facing the post-modern Church is the so-called "Church without Wall." Churches without wall are producing more and more immature Christians who have not had time to fellowship with other believers, pray or participate in the fellowship of Holy Communion. 'Church without wall' was not in God's agenda; it was an idea born out of post-modern philosophy. While the media ministry is vital to the Church, there is that need for believers to have a meeting point with God and fellowship with one another. The temple in Jerusalem was designated as the house of prayer where God and His people met to commune (John 2:16).

While the apostles took the responsibility of growing the faith of the first converts, they did not neglect their hour of prayer. To them, prayer was like daily meals. One day Peter and John were going up to the temple at around 3pm, and a cripple at the entrance of the temple asked them for money. Peter told the man they had neither silver nor gold (Acts 3:6). Peter and John gave the cripple man something better, and far greater than silver and gold.

If you live in the United Kingdom, you might think that money is the answer to every need. Some people like to work every day of the week and don't have time to meet God in fellowship. These people run after money but they forget that there are many things money cannot buy which God has freely given to us.

Peter prayed in the name of Jesus, and said to the crippled man: "*Silver or gold I do not have, but what I have I give you. In the name of Jesus Christ of Nazareth, walk* " (Acts 3:6). Peter used prayer, faith and the help of the Holy Spirit to heal this man from a crippling life. The man asked for what he wanted but God gave him what he needed through the power of prayer. God can do anything for you in prayer. Peter used the authority in the name of Jesus to heal this man.

The prayer life of the apostles was entirely different from the priests who had previously met this man in his poor condition. The apostles relied on the power of the Holy Spirit, the authority in the name of Jesus, the living Word of God, and prayer to heal and deliver people from sickness and oppression of the devil. When the priests realised that they could not have the anointing of the apostles or perform miracles through their priestly rituals, they planned to persecute and stop them from preaching the good news of Jesus.

The apostles faced fierce persecution; the only power they had to confront this persecution was the power of prayer.

> ***"On their release, Peter and John went back to their own people and reported all that the chief priests and the elders had said to them. When they heard this, they raised their voices together in prayer to God. "Sovereign Lord," they said, "you made the heavens and the earth and the sea, and everything in them. You spoke by the Holy Spirit through the mouth of your servant, our father David: "'why do the nations rage and the peoples plot in vain? The kings of the earth rise up and the rulers band together against the Lord and against his anointed one."***

Indeed Herod and Pontius Pilate met together with the Gentiles and the people of Israel in this city to conspire against your holy servant Jesus, whom you anointed. They did what your power and will had decided beforehand should happen. Now, Lord, consider their threats and enable your servants to speak your word with great boldness. Stretch out your hand to heal and perform signs and wonders through the name of your holy servant Jesus." After they prayed, the place where they were meeting was shaken. And they were all filled with the Holy Spirit and spoke the word of God boldly."

-Acts 4:23-31

The apostles and the other believers were asked to be silent and stop preaching in the name of Jesus but they refused. They knew that they were sent on a mission by God, and were proclaiming what they had seen and heard from Jesus Christ the saviour of the world. The Word of truth and the act of healing and miracles that took place in their mission could not be stopped by the threats of the Sanhedrin. The apostles decided to forge ahead with the mission but needed to pray to God about the threat they faced. They prayed to sustain their vision and determination as they relentlessly pursued their God given assignment.

The apostles praised God who created all things, the one who spoke through the prophets by the Holy Spirit, and the one who now speaks to us through His Son Jesus Christ. The threat the apostles faced from opposition did not take away the praise of God from them. They realised that God was greater than the persecution they faced. They looked at their problems from scriptural perspective so that they could pray the right prayer. They praised the Sovereign Lord who is the owner of the universe and everything in it. They realised from the scriptures that there was no threat that could stand and overcome them without the will of God. They knew that the threats of the Sanhedrin were not beyond the control of God's power. The apostles found strength in the Word of God to advance their mission in prayer and boldness.

The apostles realised that the truth cannot be stopped by human threat. They knew God is truth and that it is only the truth that can set them free. They realised the truth that the kings of the Earth and the rulers only gathered together to take their stand against the Lord and against His Anointed One. It was like the creation standing against the creator; a pot standing against the potter. What do you think will happen? Believers must realise the truth that the creator of the universe is in control of human affairs and that His plan and purposes for the salvation of the world cannot be stopped by mortal men. God cannot and will not be overcome by the global rebellion of this age.

The apostles and the believers used the power of prayer to report their oppression to the Sovereign Lord who decides the fate of the persecutors and the persecuted. Christians will always overcome in prayer and in speaking the truth when their enemies seek to use state's authority to hinder their advance. Compromising the truth is the starting point of spiritual defeat. The state has the force of law to persecute the truth as preached by the Church but God has the force of truth, and sovereign authority over the state and the law makers. The Church is able to influence the world for God by standing for the truth at all cost. The truth is the only weapon that will set the world free, the Church needs to get hold of this truth.

Obedience to the way, the truth and the life of God in a carnal world is costly. Despite persecution of the believers, God delivered them as they applied the power of prayer. The confession of God's truth about our circumstances brings courage and trust in His love and care during life challenges. During Jesus' trial moment, He applied prayer to seek God's truth about His fate. He did not pray that God should destroy his persecutors but prayed for God's will to come to pass. Jesus prayed three times that the cup of sorrow and death be taken away by God, but at the same time asked for God's will to be done and not His will.

While God released Jesus to be killed by his persecutors, they could not kill the plan of God for Jesus' resurrection and the ultimate plan of God to save the world. No wonder Jesus said*"But I will show you whom you should fear: Fear Him who, after the killing of the body, has power to throw you into hell. Yes I tell you fear Him"* (Luke 12:5).

You shouldn't fear death but fear God who has power over death. Jesus surrendered His life for God's will so that He could take it back at resurrection. The apostles learned this truth that it is only God who can handle the threat of the Sanhedrin and threat the Church had to face. They knew that this threat will only serve to advance the purposes of Jesus' mission to the world. This is why they turn over the threat to God in prayer.

The greatest concern of the apostles was not the threat of their own safety, but the advancement of their mission to the world. Their prayer points were not many; they were short, direct to the point, and powerful. O Sovereign Lord, just handle their threat and give us power and boldness to preach the Word and perform wonders by your outstretched hand. While they offered one prayer point about the threat of the Sanhedrin, they prayed three prayer points for their mission and non for their safety (Acts 4:29-30).

Some believers of this generation and even some so called preachers of the gospel have written many books and prayer points about the enemies and none about the salvation of sinners. Some believers are so fearful of the threat of Satan to the extent that they have lost the knowledge of the finished work of Jesus Christ on the Cross. Many Christians going around today have forgotten the knowledge of the truth of the gospel. Those who conducted the so called deliverance rites on believers do so out of ignorance of the Word of life and the true meaning of salvation.

If you are truly saved, you have been transferred from the kingdom of darkness into the kingdom of light (Colossians 1:13-14). The truest deliverance that you will ever need is the salvation of your soul from sin. When you are saved from sin, you are saved from Satan because he has been committing sin from the beginning. This is why the Son of God appeared to destroy the work of Satan (1 John 3:9). Believers cannot destroy the work of Satan without destroying hidden sins in their lives. The weapon of genuine deliverance is the knowledge of the truth and its application to your daily living.

The apostles and the believers knew the truth about the victory which God gave to Jesus at resurrection. They used the truth about Jesus to turn the threat of the Sanhedrin into eternal testimony. Jesus' tomb was sealed, and soldiers stood watching for how He would be resurrected. The greater and higher authority however shattered their power through an earthquake! The same higher authority sent an angel to free apostle Peter, Paul and Silas from their prisons. The apostles realised that there was a hand greater and more powerful than the council of Sanhedrin. There was an unseen hand that does what you can see. You must realise your true spiritual identity and confess it daily to Satan's harassments. You are immoveable if you trust in God and His authority in your life (Psalm 125:1).

God did not destroy the Sanhedrin but rendered their threat powerless. God gave fresh anointing to the apostles to preach the Gospel, to heal and to perform wonders and miracles. They became spirit filled vessels of honour, dealing with every opposition as they advanced the mission of Jesus. The power of prayer instils boldness and power of the Holy Spirit that conquers fears. The apostles were unshakeable and unmoveable due to the presence and power of God in their lives. They continued to preach the Word of God with boldness. You too can move your mountain of threat, opposition, and persecution by the power of the Holy Spirit and prayer.

Apostle Peter, Paul and Silas in the Prison (Acts 12:1-19; 16:25-32)

As the Church began to spread from Jerusalem to Judea and to Samaria (Acts 1:8), persecution increased with the aim to stop the early Church movement. The power of the state that sought to end Jesus' mission by condemning Him to death on the Cross was still at work. The Jewish leaders (the council of Sanhedrin) agreed with King Herod to persecute the Church. The persecution scattered the early Church headquarters in Jerusalem, Philip had started a crusade in Samaria, and Saul the chief persecuting officer had been converted.

The Church in the house of Cornelius was formed.

Ironically, the persecution was used by God to advance the expansion of the Church. At that point King Herod had arrested James the brother of John and put him to death. The Jews were happy about this and Herod also arrested Peter and put him in prison, intending to bring him out for public trial. The force of political opposition was clearly in display against Christianity. The power of the Holy Spirit was however with the apostle to spread the good news and to heal those who were oppressed with diseases and evil spirit.

The Jews were trying to protect their religious traditions, and also the Temple from being emptied because of the healing and miracles performed through the power of the Holy Spirit. The Jews therefore through their most horrific and disastrous ways tried to stop the spread of the gospel by arresting, and executing the leaders who spearheaded the expansion of the Church.

Effectively two kings and their authorities were at war-the King of kings and the kings of the Earth. When the kings of the earth gathered together to arrest, try and execute Peter, Paul and Silas, the King of kings remained silent. In case of Peter, the Church earnestly prayed to God for him (Acts 12:5). In case of Paul and Silas, they praised and prayed to God inside the prison (Acts 16:25). Herod's plan was to execute Peter as he did to James but the Church prayed for Peter's safety. The prayer of the Church provoked heavenly intervention, changed King Herod's plans and liberated Peter, Paul and Silas from the prison, restored the Church's mission and defeated the plan of Herod and his evil team. The reality of that event is that prayer changes things. Through prayer, the Church depopulates prisons, wins souls to Christ, and destroys the plans of evil gangs and spread the Word of God. Like the Apostles, you can provoke divine intervention into your situation through prayer. You can quench the fire of the enemies by the power of prayer.

We hear from the news that the United Kingdom prisons are full, yet the Church claims they have prison ministries. It appears the Church is in prison herself as it has been silenced through different kinds of controversial legislations. The state is applying her political powers through different media to weaken the power of the Church and to blow the Church off the course of the Great Commission. The emerging Church is not the one that deals with sin, but the one that covers up sin at all cost, including sacrificing the truth that sets people free from immorality. The Church is silent because the truth of the Word of God has been diluted by the modern philosophies. The power of prayer has been eroded through 21st Century cosmetic Christianity.

We now have Christianity that boast of outward appearance but lack the inward transformation. We now have a Church which prayers and teachings mainly focus on prosperity and deliverance from the enemies. It is like the Church and Satan are fighting and predicting who is going to win. The Church is not in competition with the devil but an exclusive community of Spirit-filled believers to neutralise and destroy the activities of Satan. Don't be deceived; there is no equal yoke with righteousness and wickedness, light and darkness, Christ and Belial, the temple of God and the temple of idols. God's Spirit cannot dwell in His temple and the temple of idol at the same time. You need to come out of your sin before you can pray effectively.

Paul and Silas were able to praise God in the prison because of the eternal values set before them. Billy Graham says: "Christians rejoice in the midst of persecution because they have eternity's values in view. When the pressures are on, they looked beyond their present predicament to the glories of heaven" (Billy Graham; The Secret of Happiness, page 138). You can praise God and pray to Him when you realise that God's presence is with you in any situation. You can burst into praise when you are convinced that God is greater than any problem you may face. You can turn your sadness to joy, switching on your heavens through praise and prayer, believing that God is in your situation with you and that He will fulfil His ultimate purpose for your life.

The empty cathedrals, prison congestion, widespread crime, moral decadence and the wrong that are being touted as right today all suggest that the Church has lost the power of prayer and power of the gospel of salvation. The Church must pray for genuine revival that will restore the world. It is through earnest prayer that the Church will challenge the power of the State and release the power of God to overturn the threat of opposition. There is no amount of dialogue, consultation or networking that will deal with satanic activities without the power of prayer. If Elijah alone could defeat 850 prophets of Baal, Paul and Silas opened the prison gates through prayer, we can all change the world for God through the power of prayer. Prayer is one of the most important weapons the Church has to fight the deadly threat of opposition, and the Church has to depend entirely on God for all her activities and challenges. In spite of political powers and opposition, God will continue to act on behalf of the Church till eternity.

The Witnessing Power of the Church

The witnessing power of the Church was birthed in the power of prayer (Acts 6:4; 13:1-3). The apostles and disciples of Jesus Christ waited in constant prayer (Acts 1:14). They gathered together to pray for boldness to spread the Word of God (Acts 4:29). The apostles prioritised prayer and the spread of the Word of God when there was internal conflict in the early Church (Acts 6:4). The Church of Antioch fasted and prayed and heard the voice of the Holy Spirit before sending Paul and Barnabas on their missionary journey. (Acts 13:1-3).

The apostles and the disciples of the early Church realised that true witness of the gospel of Jesus Christ centred around four principles - hearing the Word of God, obeying the Word of God, doing the Word of God, and praying the Word of God. These principles led them into revelation, consecration and communication of the Good News. The power of the Holy Spirit centred on hearing, obeying, doing and praying what the Word of God said. Jesus told the disciples: "*You will receive power when the Holy Spirit comes upon you; and you will be my witnesses in Jerusalem, and in all Judea and Samaria, and to the ends of the earth*"(Acts 1:8).What Jesus meant here is that when the apostles and disciples receive the Baptism of the Holy Spirit, they would receive the ability to hear God when He spoke as Jesus did. They would receive the ability to obey the Word of God as Jesus did when He was with them. They would receive the ability to speak the Word of God as Jesus spoke during his earthly ministry. They would also be able to confess what they heard whenever they conversed with Him in prayer. Jesus said:

> ***"The words I say to you are not just my own. Rather, it is the Father, living in me, who is doing his work. Believe me when I say that I am in the Father and the Father is in me; or at least believe on the evidence of the miracles themselves. I tell you the truth, anyone who has faith in me will do what I have been doing. He will do even greater things than these, because I am going to the Father."***
>
> ***-John 14:10-12***

The Father lives in Jesus Christ in the person of the Holy Spirit and the same promise was made by Jesus to His disciples who will carry the gospel torch to the end of the world. The power of hearing, saying, obeying, and doing the Word of God was not the product of mental or natural wisdom or philosophy but the enabling power of the Holy Spirit witnessing through the disciples. Whenever the apostles and the disciples used the power of prayer, they were in communion and dialogue with God through the indwelling Holy Spirit. They could hear the Holy Spirit telling them what to say, what to do and when to do it at every point of their ministry. Some problems you may have with your prayer life are the ability to hear, interpret and apply what God told you in prayer.

This is the account when Peter stood before the rulers and elders of the Jews:

> ***"Then Peter, filled with the Holy Spirit, said to them: Rulers and elders of the people! If we are being called to account today for an act of kindness shown to a man who was lame and are being asked how he was healed, then know this, you and all the people of Israel: It is by the name of Jesus Christ of Nazareth, whom you crucified but whom God raised from the dead, that this man stands before you healed. Jesus is the stone***

> ***you builders rejected, which has become the cornerstone.' Salvation is found in no one else, for there is no other name under heaven given to mankind by which we must be saved." When they saw the courage of Peter and John and realized that they were unschooled, ordinary men, they were astonished and they took note that these men had been with Jesus."***
>
> ***-Acts 4:8-13***

Peter informed the rulers and elders of Israel that healing was not achieved by their natural ability, but by the power of someone doing it through them. The ability to perform the miracle was given by Jesus Christ who they intended to destroy. Jesus was the stone rejected by the builders that became the chief cornerstone of the house. Peter was saying to the rulers: "We are not in this mission by our own imagination; we were sent. And He that sent us is working through us." Peter told the people that there was an unseen but real presence of God in them that mightily manifested. As the Father was in Jesus, He was in them fulfilling His divine will. If you are sent on a mission, you are not alone. God is with you and in you through His Spirit. If you commit yourself to Him, He will guide you into all truths and all the assignments He committed into your hand.

Peter said "If your rulers were asking us how this lame man was healed, we cannot experiment or explain these acts in detail. Even if we tried to explain it, you will neither understand nor believe it. It was not by medical or by surgical intervention; it was a supernatural act of God! All I can explain is that there is a name that was given to us to heal the sick, and that name is Jesus." Jesus Christ told them *"I will do whatever you ask in my name, so that the Son may bring glory to the Father. You may ask me for anything in my name and I will do it"*(John 14:13-14).

Salvation or deliverance from sin, wickedness and evil cannot be found in any other name apart from Jesus Christ. King Solomon declared:*"The name of the Lord is a strong tower; the righteous run to it and they are safe"*(Proverb 18:10). Jesus declared that He is the only way and the truth; the only life giver from God. No one can come to the Father except through Him (John 14:6). God designated Jesus to be the Saviour of the world and no one else can be His equal. This absolute truth cannot be compromised by the Church.

The only way of salvation from sin and evil of this generation is to accept Jesus as the true Saviour and Lord. There was no other religious teacher or leader who chose to die for our sins apart from the only begotten Son who rose from the dead on the third day. Jesus is the only way chosen by God to have an eternal relationship with you. There is no other name or way! Luke pointed this out:

> ***"Then he opened their minds so they could understand the Scriptures. He told them, "This is what is written: The Messiah will suffer and rise from the dead on the third day, and repentance for the forgiveness of sins will be preached in his name to all nations, beginning at Jerusalem. You are witnesses of these things. I am going to send you what my Father has promised; but stay in the city until you have been clothed with power from on high"***
>
> ***-Luke 24:45-49***

The world is not safe without the Saviour!

When the elders and rulers of the Jews saw the wisdom of Peter and John whom they regarded as ordinary men and unschooled, they were amazed about what their relationship with Jesus has done in their lives. Peter and John did not go to a rabbinic school to study Jewish theology but they had been with Jesus -'the Word that became flesh' and spoke through them. The witnessing task of the Church is not just studying theology, it is a matter of who lives in you and the amount of His revelation that you have received. When you have Jesus and His Word in your life, God's presence dwells in you. You carry God's ultimate power that holds the universe together. The devil, demons, and their activities cannot harm you. Jesus had this to say:

> ***"You are already clean because of the word I have spoken to you. Remain in me, as I also remain in you. No branch can bear fruit by itself; it must remain in the vine. Neither can you bear fruit***

unless you remain in me. "I am the vine; you are the branches. If you remain in me and I in you, you will bear much fruit; apart from me you can do nothing. If you do not remain in me, you are like a branch that is thrown away and withers; such branches are picked up, thrown into the fire and burned. If you remain in me and my words remain in you, ask whatever you wish, and it will be done for you. This is to my Father's glory, that you bear much fruit, showing yourselves to be my disciples"

-John 15: 3-8

A changed life preaches the gospel and demonstrates God's power with boldness to others than what they say. Peter was not a motivational speaker but was endowed by the Holy Spirit of God. While many motivational speakers work on the emotions of their listeners, Peter's messages became the two-edged sword that pierced into the spirit, joints and marrows, and the power that judged the thoughts and attitudes of the rulers and elders of Israel. The sword of the Law cannot withstand the sword of the Spirit but must be reinforced by the sword of the Spirit to deal with the social and spiritual evil of this age!

The power of witnessing is not in what you learn from the seminary alone but the measure of revelation of the Word of God that you have in you. You cannot become the true light of the world without radiating the light that shines in the midst of darkness. The light shines in darkness, but the darkness has not understood it (John 1:5). The moral darkness of this age can only be lightened by the light of the gospel. The Church is allowing the darkness of this age to extinguish the light of the gospel by accommodating moral decay packaged by post-modern lifestyles. The Church has put her light under the table of ungodliness, and is no more a witness against sins and its consequences.

The phrase 'inclusive or emerging church' suggests that light and darkness, righteousness and wickedness, right and wrong should live together. The new kind of Christianity has compromised with idolatry in the Church. Those who are in the camp of emerging Christianity have forgotten that the Scripture cannot be broken as Paul told us:

"Do you not know that wrongdoers will not inherit the

kingdom of God? Do not be deceived: Neither the sexually immoral nor idolaters nor adulterers nor men who have sex with men nor thieves nor the greedy nor drunkards nor slanderers nor swindlers will inherit the kingdom of God. And that is what some of you were. But you were washed, you were sanctified, you were justified in the name of the Lord Jesus Christ and by the Spirit of our God"

-1 Cor.6:9-11

"Put to death, therefore, whatever belongs to your earthly nature: sexual immorality, impurity, lust, evil desires and greed which are idolatry. Because of these, the wrath of God is coming. You used to walk in these ways; in the life you once lived."

-Colossians 3:5-7

The gospel preachers and the Church that accept moral laxities and teach others to live such lives are not true preachers of Word of God. They are the kind of teachers apostle Paul described as men and (women) who did not put up with sound doctrine but suited their own desires; the teachers who say what the itching ears want to hear, and those who turn their ears away from the truth (2 Timothy 4:3-4). The Word of God is what God has said, what He is saying through His Prophets, and not what we think He has said or saying through our post-modern philosophy.

Paul the Apostle revealed the origin of two kinds of gospel:

"I am astonished that you are so quickly deserting the one who called you to live in the grace of Christ and are turning to a different gospel— which is really no gospel at all. Evidently some people are throwing you into confusion and are trying to pervert the gospel of Christ. But even if we or an angel from heaven should preach a gospel other than the one we preached to you, let them be under God's curse! As we have already said, so now I say again: If anybody is preaching to you a gospel other than what you accepted, let them be under God's curse! Am I now trying to win the approval of human beings, or of God? Or am I trying to please people? If I were still trying to please people, I would not be a servant of Christ. I want you

to know, brothers and sisters that the gospel I preached is not of human origin. I did not receive it from any man, nor was I taught it; rather, I received it by revelation from Jesus Christ." -Galatians 1:6-12.

Apostle Paul spoke about another gospel that threw his converts into confusion; the kind of gospel that was not given by Jesus Christ. Those people that preach inclusive gospel are preaching another gospel. It is as simple as that! If the gospel and the Church are inclusive, then there is no need for condemning sin, no need for salvation, no need for repentance and definitely no need for holiness. The gospel that Jesus preached was exclusive gospel and the life He lived was an exclusive life. Jesus desired the Church to be an exclusive community where the wounded world would be healed. The Church is producing another Scripture, another kind of Christianity, another church, and another 'Jesus' which arises from the god of the mind. But the Church needs to preach the Word of truth to the lost for the world to be saved. The true gospel is the basis of true prayer life. When the gospel is distorted, Christian prayer life is mis-guided and prayer points are mis-fired. You need the knowledge of true Word of God in order to pray according to God's will.

POINTS ON PRAYER

- The power of prayer instils boldness and power of the Holy Spirit that conquers fears.
- You can praise God and pray to Him when you realise that God's presence is with you in any situation.
- The true gospel is the basis of true prayer life.

Chapter 12

Use the Power of Prayer

WE LIVE IN an age where reason and knowledge seem to be the only source of answers to human problems. Post-modern thinking is affecting the spiritual realities of many people in the world today. Humanity wants the shortest and the quickest ways to find answers to their problems. These world views have led to certain discoveries and developments that are closing the door of human hearts to realities of the powers and the existence of God. The world is full of sickness, pain, distress, depression, poverty, loneliness, hopelessness, bareness, persecution, divorce, hatred, economic crises, inequality, oppression, killing, crime, horrific acts, deceit and loss of loved ones, property, business, savings, and death. Good and evil will continue to exist until Jesus Christ comes back.

> ***"Is any one of you in trouble? He or she should pray. The prayer of the righteous is powerful and effective."***
>
> ***-James 5:1, 16***

How can you handle a world where you don't even know what the next agenda for your life is? James advises that you should pray if you are in any of these troubles. Do you know why? You need to present your troubles to the one who knows everything about them and the one who has answers to the problems. When you give God all your troubles, you will be surprised that He has answers to every challenge in your life. Jesus told his disciples:

> ***"I am coming to you now, but I say these things while I am still in the world, so that they may have the full measure of my joy within them. I have given them your word and the world has hated them, for they are not of the world any more than I***

> ***am of the world. My prayer is not that you take them out of the world but that you protect them from the evil one. They are not of the world, even as I am not of it. Sanctify them by the truth; your word is truth."***
>
> ***-John 17:13-17***

Jesus talked about two worlds in this passage: the world we live in and the world where God lives. Heaven or the kingdom of God is the realm where God dwells. Jesus said the disciples were in the world but they were not of the world and not under the control of the world. Jesus had given them the Word of truth and it has set them free from errors. By this Word, they had realised that God, Jesus Christ and the Holy Spirit of God are real, and exist in heaven and in the hearts of those who believe in Him. The Word, the Spirit and the prayer of fellowship must keep the disciples connected with the throne of grace.

Jesus Christ connected Heaven and Earth through prayer, and He teaches us to always start our prayer by hallowing our Father in heaven. God protected Jesus from troubles of His time, from being killed by Herod, from arrest by His countrymen and from decay in the grave. No wonder He declared to His disciples and the Church that 'all authority in heaven and on earth has been given to me; I am with you till the end of the age'.

When Jesus Christ gave the Word to His disciples, He gave them God. In the beginning was the Word and the Word was with God and the Word was God (John 1:1). The Word He gave them was not just the written code of the law of the Jews, but the Word of Spirit and life (John 6:63). By that Word, Jesus sanctified the disciples, who were set apart to relate with God, and proclaim God to the lost world. Jesus said by this Word we have eternal life (John 17:3) and the eternal life is the knowledge of God as the only true God.

The question in the mind of this age is that if God exists, why did He allow evil and troubles in our lives? What many failed to ask is whether God is able to deal with the evil in our world. A mind disconnected from the creator is prone to do evil which is set to continue to increase in our world. The best way to deal with evil is to transform the mind of human being through the manual of God's written Word. The Psalmist declared *"He sent forth his word and healed them; He rescued them from the grave"*(Psalm 107:20). Any product that is used without the manufacturer's manual will have fault due to misuse. A faulty mind cannot heal a hurt mind. The greatest fault of the post-modern thinking is the disconnection of the human mind from its creator, which is bound to be faulty.

Since the human mind is inherently faulty, troubles will continue to abound. The human mind needs to be renewed and restored, and reconnected to its maker. Jesus came into the world to do just that. Prayer requires a faith that believes that God exists, and the starting point is the true knowledge of whom you are dialoguing with. Prayer is never an abstract relationship or conversation; it is a relationship with the living God. You need the Word of God and prayer to clean your mind from daily spiritual contaminations. The power of prayer is from God's authority given to you in the name of Jesus. It requires faith in God, the presence and power of the Holy Spirit in you, and the presence of His creative Word in you.

As you have journeyed through this book, you have learnt how various people used the power of prayer at various times for various needs. Moses the Prophet interceded for the Israel Nation; Joshua prayed for victory over wars with neighbouring nations; and Hannah prayed for a child at Shiloh. Daniel also prayed against mass murder, for insight to interpret the King's dreams and to receive deep revelations, to be delivered from the Lion's den, and for Israel's liberation from slavery. Jesus prayed for the sick, the demon possessed, and for the salvation of the world. The early Church prayed against persecution, for their deliverance, for their mission and for the courage to spread the Word of God. All these prayer giants saw the need to discuss their personal, domestic, community, political, social, ethical or economic challenges and problems with God through prayer. They all believed that God is the one who has answers.

MY EXPERIENCE OF POWER OF PRAYER

Iwas born and grew up in a pagan family. My father was a peasant farmer and we used to live in a hut in the local farm. I never saw the Bible or my parents pray until I got converted. During my early years, I remembered I had a sickness which was so terrible that my parents lost every hope that I would survive. There was no access to hospitals or medical treatment near our farm. My parents depended on herbal medicine for treatment and healing. My father tried every medicine but none worked. As my parents were awaiting the worst possible scenario, a woman who came from a nearby farm to visit my father saw the situation I was in and the helplessness facing my parents. This woman prescribed a particular herb that my father used to cure my illness. The traditional medicine worked and I was completely healed.

I became a born again Christian after my secondary school education in 1987. As a young convert from an unbelieving family, I associated myself with believers from a local church. I followed them to church, fellowship and prayer meetings. We were at a night vigil prayer meeting one day. I saw a revelation in the form of a trance. I saw a man in a white garment whose head reached the heaven but I couldn't see His face. The man took hold of my hand and asked me to follow him. As I followed him on a narrow road, we got to a junction where the road divided into two. We walked down the left side of the road and came to a very dark space. The man in the white garment dropped the needle in his hand and asked me to pick it for him. I told him I couldn't see the needle because of the thick darkness. He then bent down and picked the needle and we walked back to the junction. We walked down the right side of the road and came to a very big space full of light. This light made the man's white garment glitter such that I couldn't look at his garment any longer. He dropped the same needle and asked me to pick it for him and I did as I could see the needle because of the great light.

The man took me back to the junction on the road and told me that those were the two ways in the world and that I should make up my mind the way I wanted to walk for the rest of my life. I then came back to my senses and realised that I was in the midst of believers praying at a night vigil. I was so baffled with this revelation that I couldn't pray again that night.

As I thought about that vision, I was disturbed in my heart as I didn't know what it meant. I visited the church's prophet and narrated the vision to him, hoping to be given an explanation. The prophet prayed for me and told me that the man I saw in that revelation was Jesus and He loved me and He wanted me to follow His way. Since then, I made up my mind to give my life to Him, to obey His Word and to do His will.

This vision marked the beginning of a new era in my life as a new Christian. Jesus said: *"Enter by the narrow gate; for wide is the gate and broad is the way that leads to destruction, and there are many who go in by it. Because narrow is the gate and difficult is the way which leads to life, and there are few who find it"* (Matthew 7:13-14). The power of prayer unveils the package of your future, opens your heavens and delivers God's programme to you.

I decided to dedicate my life to God, and His love grew in my heart continually. I told my friends I wanted to follow Jesus Christ and forsake the world. Jesus inspired me and I joined the church's prayer team, the choir and the Sunday school to grow spiritually. I later noticed that I had developed an uncontrollable passion for the Word of God. I studied the Bible more than any other book and listened to the preaching of anointed men of God. It was the tradition of the local church during that period, to teach, prepare and fellowship together every Thursday to wait for the baptism of the Holy Spirit, and we fasted and met in the evenings to study the Bible. I attended this 'tarry' meeting for about six months before I received the baptism of the Holy Spirit.

While waiting, I had other revelations which I want to share with you. One day, I came from a tarry meeting, ended my fast and went to sleep. I dreamt that two brothers were praying for me as I knelt in their midst. A white dove flew from heaven, and rested on my right shoulder; and flew back to heaven again. I woke up from my sleep and felt that my mouth was bitter as if I have just eaten cola nut.

While I was meditating on this revelation, a voice in my heart said to me that if I wanted to receive the baptism of the Holy Spirit, I have to give up smoking cigarettes and eating cola nuts. I started praying immediately for His grace to forsake these habits. During that time, we had seven days of fasting and prayer in my local church. On the seventh day, I had another revelation and I saw Late Apostle Joseph Ayodele Babalola, the founder of Christ Apostolic Church in the sky with white doves flying around him. I sensed a gentle breeze around me and woke up speaking in tongues. I started worshipping and praising God before we started the vigil and I realised that I could not continue speaking in tongue as I expected.

The power of prayer prepares your heart for the divine visitation of the Holy Spirit, who enables you to pray ceaselessly. Prayer changes the course of your life and connects you to God's divine plan and purpose. The power of prayer gives you the right direction to life, the right way out of difficulties and victory over unseen forces. The power of prayer connects you to the sanctuary of God's blessings and the original agenda of God for your life. The power of prayer connects you with the divine presence of God and heals you from fear of the unknown. The power of prayer brightens your future and open doors of opportunities for you. The power of prayer will change your story forever.

As I waited for the baptism of the Holy Spirit, I had the expectation that I would receive the gift one day. I continued in my regular fellowship in the local church and participated in church activities. One day we were in choir practice. Our choir master was very strict and a disciplinarian. He admonished one boy who was not serious during the session and he made comments generally about the boys in the choir, of which I was one. This comment that we boys in the choir are looking for girlfriends made me so angry to the extent that I thought of leaving the choir. I thought about this matter for a week, and sought advice from people about what to do as I did not want to experience a recurrence.

I was preparing for a Friday night vigil prayer meeting and was serious thinking about leaving the choir. As I pondered before the vigil started, I heard a voice within me that told me that in order to receive the baptism of the Holy Spirit and serve Him, I should forget about the incident and remain in the choir. It was like someone entered my heart and blew off the thought, and I had the peace of God in my heart. That same night, the Holy Spirit came upon me in power and I spoke in tongues and prophesy for almost one hour during the prayer meeting. Since then, the Spirit of God dwells in me, manifesting His grace in me and through me as He wills.

This has continued to teach me lessons on sanctification and forgiveness and inspired me to commit my life to His will. He has also helped me to pray more and also fellowship. I now realise at this point the need to completely depend on Him for all the challenges of life. So I became the first Christian in my family. The Holy Spirit and sin cannot live in the same place. The power of the Holy Spirit conquers self in your heart. The Holy Spirit gives you desire for holiness, love of God and passion for prayer. The Holy Spirit delivers His gifts and fruits into your life. He reveals deeper things to you in prayer.

My Experience at the higher institution

When I gained admission into a higher institution in 1990, my father knew that I had become a Christian but he was not. He believed in voodoo powers, which is also called juju in some parts of Africa. He advised me not to go to college without the help of juju power to protect me from evil. At that time, I had renounced the power of *'Aiyelala'*- the juju power that protects someone from harm. I had thrown away the Ayelala's ring that my father gave me and my father knew that the only power I relied on then was the power of the Almighty God. My father tried to persuade me that it was God who gave traditional priests the power to invoke powers over evil but I told my father that the power of God did not need support from man to work. The power of God lives in you if you believe in Jesus Christ as your Lord and Saviour. I was radical with my faith then and I challenged my father 'if I go to the higher institution and I do not finish my course or fail to come back alive, that means God does not exist. My father couldn't say anything else, and that faith confession settled the whole matter.

I left for the higher institution with my Bible, my hymn book and my prayer life. I never knew that I was challenging my father and my entire family. As I left my father, I heard the voice of the Holy Spirit say to me, 'I will surely protect you but you will need to pray fervently when you get to school. With this warning, the first thing I did was to join a local church fellowship on campus. I was welcomed and I felt at home; we fellowshipped together regularly and went to a local church in the city on Sundays and Friday nights for vigil prayers.

I was elected as the prayer secretary for the campus fellowship in 1992. I had several spiritual encounters during this time; one was a dream revelation where I was critically sick at the campus and was admitted into the campus clinic. While I was awaiting the doctor, I saw a man dressed in white linen came to me and laid his hand on me and prayed. He told me I was healed and that I should leave the clinic and go home. When I woke up the next day, I had a big blister in my mouth at night that was healed instantly in the morning, which I did not have when I went to bed. Those who saw me the following day started asking me where I had an accident. I told them I did not have any accident and that I had woken up and found the mark in my mouth. Throughout my stay on campus, I never attended the campus clinic for treatment and I was not sick for one day.

The power of God sustained me throughout my studies and that power which was the same yesterday, today and forevermore sustained me till the present time. My entire family later gave their lives to Jesus and became Christians. God's power is enough to protect you and provide for all your needs. The power of prayer connects you with the presence of God; helps you to tap into the domain of God's spiritual blessings and sustain you through the storms of life. You can live heaven on earth if you have faith in God and know how to commune with Him in prayer.

One day after a Friday night vigil prayer meeting, I experienced an uncommon visitation of the Holy Spirit and I prophesied for two hours. Most of these prophecies came to pass within a short time. After the vigil, I had a revelation that I was in the midst of the 12 apostles and Jesus was standing with us in the upper room of an apartment. Jesus held a book that contained the names of Christians in the world, and confirmed to me that my name was there. He held fresh palm leaves in His hand and said "I will be touching all of you on the head with this palm leaves and on whoever a seed fell upon has been chosen as a prophet to the nations." As I opened my eyes in this dream, I saw a white seed on my cloth, and Jesus said to me, "I have chosen you as a prophet to the nations." I said to myself, "I will take the seed and preserve it because if I planted it then, people will uproot it." Then I woke up from my sleep. I documented this revelation and started praying and meditating about it.

I received other similar revelations before I finished my higher education. I later applied for jobs to support my family and to sponsor my brothers' education to higher institutions. While I was praying, God revealed something different from what I had in mind. God had another agenda for me. I had a dream revelation in which I saw a newly cultivated farm. In the middle of this farm was a glass house where the owner of the farm was living. When the man saw me, he asked me whether I was looking for a job. I said 'yes.' He asked me to work for him by planting yam seed on the heaps. I said 'okay' but I knew within my heart that this was not the kind of job I was looking for. I ignored the vision and continued to pray for the job I wanted. As I continued in my prayer, I had another dream revelation that I had a yam plantation in my home town. This yam plantation was very leafy and green, suggesting that I would have a great harvest that year. Suddenly there was a heavy rain which washed away the entire yam plantation and the heaps. Then I woke up.

As I was meditating and praying on this revelation, I heard the Holy Spirit within me say 'if you do any work apart from the work I asked you to do, what happened to the yam plantation will happen to you.'

At this time, I had forgotten the commission I had when I was at the college. This message prompted me to go into seven days continuous fasting and prayer. The Lord revealed other things to me and I gave up looking for job to embark on God's assignment. God asked me to meditate on the parable of the rich young man (Matthew 19:16-29). This Scripture turned my attention from worldly treasures to heavenly treasures. I realised that there is no perfection in possession, and I made up my mind to study Theology in 1993. That decision marked the beginning of planting the seed given to me.

Every human being travels in two major paths - the part of self-will and the path of God's will. The path of self will always conflict with the path of God's will. It takes the power of prayer and the Word of God to discern the plans and purposes of God for your life. You should not live a life based on trial and error principle. God has a definite plan for your life and you can get this plan by using the power of prayer. Prayer is not about presenting your desire to God but it is about searching for God's desire for your life. Prayer is not a spiritual gambling but gaining access to God's heart to get His original plan for you.

POINTS ON PRAYER

- Prayer requires a faith that believes that God exists.
- The power of prayer prepares your heart for the divine visitation of the Holy Spirit.
- The power of prayer gives you the right direction to life.

Chapter 13

Prayer Works

I LOVEDPRAYINGAS a new Christian and prayer had been my normal practice since I received the baptism of the Holy Spirit. I was called by God through prayer and passion for studying the Word of God regularly. I planned my ministerial mission out of nothing except faith in God, His Word and prayer. As a young graduate doing my industrial attachment at Ajaokuta Steel Complex, Nigeria, I received an appointment letter to work in the same company in 1992. I turned down this offer to pursue my ministerial assignment. I had no money or sponsor and I had surrendered myself to be used by God. I told my father that was what God told me to do. My father found it hard to believe and he tried to convince me that ministers of the gospel are poor people, and that if I followed that cause, I will remain poor for the rest of my life. But from what I have read in the Scriptures given to me by the Holy Spirit, I realised that I wasn't going to be poor for obeying the call of God. After much persuasion, he let me alone to do what I wanted but I knew he was not happy with my decision.

I started praying, fasting and studying the Word of God for guidance. As I was praying and planning, my father realised that I meant business. He asked me "Where are you going to get money to go to the seminary?" I told him straight away that God will provide. My father gave me 100 Naira in Nigerian money which is equivalent to around 45 pence according to current exchange rate to buy some food stuff to take to the seminary. I immediately went to a Christian bookshop in my home town and used the money to buy a book titled 'The Preacher and his Preaching' by Alfred Gibbs. I was left with no money but I believed as I prayed for my school fees and money for feeding and transportation.

While I continued in my prayer, I had a dream revelation that I travelled to the seminary where I saw lots of new Naira (Nigerian currency) notes in my pocket and went to the administrative office to pay my school fees for the whole three years course duration. When I checked the remaining money, I was sure that I had enough money to cater for myself at the seminary. Later, I saw two white men whom I have never seen physically till today at the seminary. They told me they had been looking for me and that I should go home and pack my luggage to attend the seminary. Then I woke up.

A man who knew that I had been called into the work of God gave me my first year school fees. God used other people to support me financially including my father who had refused initially. God started to build my faith and trust in Him for all my needs, and throughout my three years stay at the seminary, God provided for me beyond my expectations. It is true that God gives us our daily bread if we can trust Him on daily basis and pray to Him for our needs. The power of prayer requires total trust and dependence on God for all you need for life. The power of prayer opens the sanctuary of God's provisions, connect you with the people He has ordained to bless and support you and open doors of opportunities for you in a miraculous way. God will never call you to embark on an assignment He has not made provision for. He is an all sufficient God.

During my first year in the seminary, I had a serious attack that led to sickness. Whenever I coughed, I vomited blood continuously. I prayed and believed God would heal me. One day, we were having evening hostel fellowship and I heard a voice saying to me "Do you know that you will die at midnight today and your corpse will be taken to your home town tomorrow?" I responded by quoting Psalm 118:17 *"I will not die but live, and will proclaim what the Lord has done."* We finished the fellowship and went to bed to sleep without fear. The voice melted away from my heart like snow in the sun, and the peace of God flowed within my heart.

At midnight in my dream revelation, I heard the principal singing seven victorious hymns from our gospel hymn book, and prayed.

Later, I saw someone shooting a gun at me in my dream. As I was picking up the bullets from my linen cover, I woke up. From that day, I started recovering from that sickness miraculously and I was completely healed without going to the hospital. The Psalmist says *"He sent out his Word and healed them; he rescued them from the grave"*(Psalm 107:20). There is power in the Word of God and prayer. God made His Word real to me.

In 1992, I had a terrible sickness that started before we were about to have a three days fast and prayer in my local church. I was so sick that my mother advised me not to attend the programme. But within my mind, I resolved that nothing will stop me from attending the programme. The following day, I packed my luggage and joined the prayer warriors. As I entered the church at 12 mid-day, a gentle and cool breeze blew all over my body at the door step. I sensed within my spirit that this was not an ordinary breeze. Immediately I felt an unusual strength within me to fast and pray, which I did for the three days. Since that day, I have never experienced such terrible sickness. The Word of God and the power of prayer are strong weapons of healing and deliverance from sickness. You can be healed from your chronic and long term illness by your faith in God, His Word and prayer.

This is how God works through prayer: Jesus said "*Ask and it will be given to you; seek and you will find; knock and the door will be opened for you. For everyone who ask receives; he who seeks finds; and to him who knocks, the door will be opened"* (Matthew 7:7-8). This Scripture was made real to me throughout my entire prayer life.

I remembered a time when I was in my second year in the seminary and I had run out of money and food. I wanted to sort myself out without praying. There was a part-time job at the seminary involving the construction of new auditorium. Students were asked to manually fill the foundation level with red soil and were to be paid at the end of the day. I quickly applied for the job so that I can get some money to buy food. While working, I heard the Holy Spirit ask me: "Is this what I asked you to do when you lack money and food?" I couldn't respond to the question other than to say "Holy Spirit I am sorry."

I left the job at that point without taking any money for the work I have done. I prayed that day and waited for God to provide. The following day, one of my friends that heard that I was in the seminary came to visit me for the first time. He took me out and did shopping for me and gave me money to buy the things I needed. He gave me his address and asked me to come to him whenever I ran out of money. That was how God provided for me at the time. The secret of lack is not because God cannot provide for your needs; it is because you failed to ask God for your needs. Jesus declared: *"Which of you fathers, if your son asks fora fish, will give him a snake instead? Or if he asks for an egg, will give him a scorpion? If you then, though you are evil, know how to give good gifts to your children, how much more will your Father in heaven give the Holy Spirit to those who ask Him!"* (Luke 11:11-13). Like Jabez, you can put your life in order through the power of prayer.

After my seminary training, I was to get married before I could be posted to the local church to work as an assistant pastor according to my church tradition. I had been praying continually for God's choice of a woman that would be suitable for me in the ministry. I remember I prayed for marriage for six years!

God's Own Choice

I had come across several ladies that we usually called 'sisters' in the college and my church. Personally I had my preference for the type of a lady I would like to marry - someone light in complexion. My father had also advised me that I should marry from my village according to our local custom. I therefore had three choices to present to God in prayer-my personal choice, my father's choice and God's choice. One night, I had a dream revelation about a lady I had lived with in the mission house for almost two years. I had never thought that she would be my wife and I had never discussed marriage with her at any time. I dreamt that this lady fried some eggs and we ate together and went to sleep in the same bed and I woke up. I did not understand this dream, and I asked myself "Could this be God's choice of wife for me?"

I shared this revelation with my senior pastor who asked me if I knew the lady in the real life. I said 'yes'. My pastor advised me that she would be my future wife but that I should pray, share the vision with her and ask her to pray about it. I met the lady and told her what I dreamt about and asked her to pray about it. Within my heart, I knew she was not light in complexion, and she was not even from my village. If she is God's choice, how would I inform my parents and introduce her to them? All these questions turned around within my head.

Finally the lady confirmed God's will that we were to be a couple. We started our courtship, prayed together and received counselling from our pastor. I introduced the lady to my parents and they accepted God's will without controversy. God also confirmed His will to the parents of this lady. We planned our marriage within six month without any savings but God was faithful to His promises. She has been a wonderful gift from God for the past 18 years.

I and my wife were posted to my first church as an assistant pastor after we got married. God blessed us with a baby boy but on the sixth day, the child died. It was a real blow to us as a young couple. There are many interpretations to such a sad event in Africa. Some people said my wife was a witch and that the child died because she didn't want to have a baby with me. During this sorrowful and confusing state, I went into three days fasting and prayer to ask God why He allowed the child to die. I shared this plan with my wife and went to our church to seek the face of God for answers. On the third day, I heard the Holy Spirit within me saying 'I took the child from you because you loved him more than me.' I started meditating on this inner voice as I was sure that God was responding to my questions.

I began to reflect on my love for the child, and the place this child took in my heart. I realised God was true. The Spirit of God took me to the story of Abraham and Isaac in Genesis 22:1-15. At that point, I confessed my sin and prayed to God to heal me from selfishness. There is nothing wrong about having a child but when the love of what you can get from God is all you think about and not the love of God who gives children, it is a sin. Then I prayed to God, I want you to restore this child back to me as I have determined to love you more than anything I possessed in life so that people may know that you are the only God that can kill and bring back to life. The Spirit of God gave me Genesis 1:28 as confirmation to my prayers: "*And God bless them, and God said unto them, be fruitful and multiply, and replenish the earth, and subdue it, and have dominion over the fish of the sea and over the fowl of the air, and over every living thing that move upon the earth.*" God confirmed His Word in our lives; my wife got pregnant, and gave birth to a set of twins - two boys. God restored our loss back to us in a wonderful way.

Dear readers, prayer works! What I learned from this incident was that in moment of hopelessness and despair, God is closer to us than any human. He is willing to speak mysteries to our hopeless situation if we can turn our heart to Him in prayer and study of His Word. Abraham called upon Him when the promised child was not forth coming (Genesis 15:1-6). Moses called Him at the Red Sea when there was no way forward (Exodus 14:13-15). Hannah cried to Him for a child; David called upon Him from the cave, Jonah cried to Him from the fish's belly; Jabez prayed to Him for blessing; King Hezekiah called for deliverance from Assyrian war and God answered them all. There is always a way out of despair if you can call upon the name of the Lord. Paul the Apostle confirmed that "*Everyone who calls upon the name of the Lord will be saved*" (Romans 10:13). I have learned the lesson of seeking God in prayer whenever there is any challenge confronting me. You too can call on Him today.

In the Ministry

Over the years, I have developed the habit of praying to God for my needs and the ministry God has committed into my hands. The Church where I served is a praying Church. We were taught to pray for everything we need and to depend on God totally. And it works! Through prayers, many deep revelations about the future were given, many battles were won, and guidance and direction were received over sensitive issues. The work of ministry requires intense prayer and study of the Word. The apostles gave their attention to prayer and the ministry of the Word (Acts 6:6). The 'Word' is God who gives His ministers what to preach. The Word of God is not the product of head knowledge. It is a bundle of revelation from God written by Spirit - filled men of God. Jesus said, *"The words I say to you I do not speak on my own authority. Rather, it is the Father, living in me, who is doing his work"* (John 14:10). The secret of receiving revelation from God and His Word is to pray. The Word of God incubated by prayer is the Word that is full of power, healing and deliverance.

In 1996, I was posted to my first church as an assistant pastor after my graduation and marriage. I went to Babalola Memorial Camp to pray and seek the face of God on what He wants me to do at this station. I planned to spend seven days before the Lord. One evening, around 7pm after finishing my prayer for the day, I went to the restaurant to break my fast for that day. I met a woman I had never seen before with one of my mates at the seminary who came to pray as well. As we were eating, the woman asked me "Why don't you buy meat with your food?" I asked her why she was asking me such a question but she kept quiet. My mate later told me the woman was a prophetess and that the reason why she probably asked such question was because she had a message from the Lord for me.

When I next saw the woman I greeted her and asked her again why she asked me the question in the restaurant. She said to me, the Spirit of God had instructed her to ask me the question that Jesus had asked His disciples in Matthew 16:14; 'who do you say I am?' I asked her what that meant. She said 'you did not see or recognise yourself the way God sees or recognise you.' This implies that I did not know my worth in God. She went further to tell me some messages about the church I was praying about, the time I will spend at this church, the next city I will move to for the ministry and how I would later travel abroad for ministerial assignment. I wrote this message down in my diary. The messages came to pass in 1997 and 2003.

There were other miracles of healing, deliverance, divine provisions, deep revelations and blessings that God has bestowed upon me and my family and the ministry through prayers. I have seen people with chronic illnesses healed, barren women giving birth to children, jobless people got good jobs, people delivered from evil powers; souls delivered from sin and Satan; evil plans terminated; battles won; marriages and broken homes restored. The power of prayer in the ministry unveils God's agenda for your ministry, connects you with God's power and provisions, shows you what God wanted to do through you and how He will do it. You can open your heavens through the power of prayer.

Jesus used prayer to conquer death (Hebrew 5:8-9) and Satan (Luke 4:1-12), Elijah prayed to deliver his own nation from idolatry, Hannah prayed to God to open her womb, Joshua prayed to uncover the secret of victories, Daniel prayed to avert bloodshed and the mouth of lions were shut and Paul and Silas prayed and the prison gates were opened. Surely God answers prayers! You too can deal with any problems in your life through the power of prayer. If you know God through His Word and you relate with Him in holiness and communal fellowship, He has answers to all your life problems and the only way to discover such answers is to give yourself to the study of God's Word and fellowship with Him in prayer. My prayer today is that God will give you a deep revelation of Himself, and that your prayer life will not remain the same. Amen.

Selected Bibliography

Selected Bibliography

Alastair Campbell;*The Story we Live By; A Reader's Guide to the New Testament*; Oxford: The Bible Reading Fellowship, 2004.

Barton & Muddiman;*The Oxford Bible Commentary*; New York: OUP, 2001

Billy Graham;*The Secret of Happiness*; USA: W Publishing Group, 2002.

Charles Spurgeon;*Prayer and Spiritual Warfare*; USA: Whitaker House, 1998.

Daniel G. Reid;*Dictionary of the New Testament*; England: IVP, 2004

Daryl Eldridge;*The Teaching Ministry of The Church: Integrating Biblical Truth with Contemporary Application*; USA: Broadman & Holman, 1995

David Yonggi Cho;*Prayer that Brings Revival*; USA: Charisma House, 1998.

Dennis C. Duling;*The Kingdom of God and the Teaching of Jesus;* New York: Word & World, Luther Seminary, 1982.

D.R. Workman;*Pray with Focus*; Australia: Big Red Rock Publishing, 2006.

Everett Ferguson;*Background of Early Christianity*; Michigan: William B. Eerdmans Publishing Company, 2003

James Luther Mays;*Psalms Interpretation: A Bible commentary for Teaching and Preaching;* USA: John Knox Press, 1994.

Loius Berkhof;*Systematic Theology*; Great Britain: Banner of Truth Trust, 2003.

Marshall I.H.;*New Testament Bible Dictionary*; England: IVP 1996

Marshall. I.H. & Co.;*New Bible Dictionary*, Illinois:; IVP, 2000

Myles Munroe;*Understanding Prayer*; USA: Whitaker House Publishing, 2001.

Norman Perrin;*The Kingdom of God in the Teachings of Jesus;* Philadelphia: Westminster Press, 1963

Wayne Grudem;*Bible Doctrines*; England: IVP, 1999.

Wesley L. Duewel;*Touch the World through Prayer*; Michigan: Zondervan Publishing House, 1986.

William Whiston;*The works of Josephus*; Complete and Unabridged, USA: Hendrickson Publishers, 1987.

About the Author

PASTOR VICTOR SULAIMAN serves as the pioneering pastor of Christ Apostolic Church Reformation Chapel based in London United Kingdom. He has been sent to impart lives with the truth of God's Word and prayer. Born again in 1987 in Christ Apostolic Church, Pastor Sulaiman was called into ministry in 1993 and became an ordained pastor in 2001. He holds a Master's degree in biblical theology. He is a dynamic teacher, conference speaker, a prophet and a Christian writer commissioned to impart the Church for meaningful Christian living and mission around the world. He has written two books titled *Holy Ghost Revival - the Greatest Need of This Millennium* and *Holy Spirit Baptism* and these have blessed many souls around the world.

Pastor Victor Sulaiman has a burden for supporting the poor, the sick and sinners to come to the knowledge of salvation and new life in Christ Jesus. He currently serves as a Healthcare Chaplain in London, United Kingdom. His powerful messages of truth, holiness and prayer life has touched many people. Pastor Victor is blessed with a loving wife and three children.

OVERCOMERS' PRAYER CONFERENCE

You are invited to join our monthly Overcomers' Prayer Conference - an interdenominational prayer retreat for all.

For more information: call us on +44(0)7897342777

E-mail: cacukrc2007@yahoo.co.uk